The MOVE Crisis in Philadelphia

The MOVE Crisis in Philadelphia

Extremist Groups and Conflict Resolution

Hizkias Assefa
and
Paul Wahrhaftig

University of Pittsburgh Press

Published 1990 by the University of Pittsburgh Press, Pittsburgh, Pa. 15260

Extremist Groups and Conflict Resolution: The MOVE Crisis in Philadelphia, by Hizkias Assefa and Paul Wahrhaftig, was originally published by Praeger Publishers, New York, a division of Greenwood Press, Inc. Copyright © 1988 by Hizkias Assefa and Paul Wahrhaftig. University of Pittsburgh Press edition by permission of the authors and Praeger Publishers.

Baker & Taylor International, London

Manufactured in the United States of America

Library of Congress Cataloging-in-Publication Data

Assefa, Hizkias.
    [Extremist groups and conflict resolution]
    The MOVE crisis in Philadelphia: extremist groups and conflict resolution / Hizkias Assefa and Paul Wahrhaftig.
        p. cm.
    Reprint. Originally published: Extremist groups and conflict resolution. New York: Praeger, 1988.
    Includes bibliographical references.
    ISBN 0-8229-5430-3
    1. MOVE (Organization) 2. Black nationalism—Pennsylvania—Philadelphia 3. Afro-Americans—Pennsylvania—Philadelphia. 4. Philadelphia (Pa.)—Race relations. 5. Conflict management—Pennsylvania—Philadelphia. I. Wahrhaftig, Paul. II. Title.
F158.N4A87   1990
974.8'1100496073—dc20   89-39454
                                                                        CIP

*To our parents
and those who see light
in the darkness.*

Contents

Photographs

List of Acronyms

CCCHR	Citywide Community Coalition for Human Rights, (Citywide Coalition for Human Rights, Citywide Black Community for Human Rights)
CIN	Crisis Intervention Network
CIP	City Intervention Program
CRS	Community Relations Service
PEHRC	Powelton Emergency Human Rights Committee
PUN	Powelton United Neighbors
RHU	Restrictive Housing Unit, "the hole"

Acknowledgments

This book would not have been possible without many people's cooperation and assistance. We would like to thank the Conflict Resolution Center, Inc., for originating the idea of undertaking this study. The Center is a worldwide resource located in Pittsburgh, Pennsylvania, dedicated to helping people successfully resolve neighborhood, racial, ethnic, or religious conflicts. Its directors were concerned that while there was much criticism when Philadelphia police bombed MOVE headquarters, there was little systematic analysis that explored other ways of handling this and similar conflicts. Thus arose the idea to do this study.

This book started as a background report for a conference of Philadelphia leadership held on the first anniversary of the MOVE bombing. The meeting was organized by the Fellowship Commission of Philadelphia and the Conflict Resolution Center, and was attended by city officials, police officers, and community leaders. The report served as a background working paper to aid participants in developing strategies to handle future conflicts of a similar nature.

An internationally recognized panel of conflict resolution experts was convened to analyze and comment on the report. It included Ms. Laura Blackburne, director of the Institute for Mediation and Conflict Resolution in New York City; Dr. James H. Laue, director of the Conflict Clinic, University of Missouri;

and Dr. Christopher Mitchell, of the Conflict Research Group, City University of London. Their contribution was crucial in helping participants in the conference think through ways to develop more effective conflict-resolution processes to handle future MOVE-type situations or other difficult community problems. We thank these panelists for their criticism as well as for their support and encouragement to develop this book. Furthermore, we would like to express our gratitude to the Allen Hilles Fund and the Anna H. and Elizabeth M. Chace Fund for financing the early phases of this research.

Many people were interviewed to gather the information for this book, including third-party intervenors, representatives of the Philadelphia administration in the 1970s, MOVE members, and their neighbors. We are deeply grateful for their time and their willingness to share their views and perspectives with us.

It was not possible to interview representatives of the Goode administration because of a pending grand jury investigation of the 1985 bombing. However, during the research period, Mayor Goode had established a Special Investigation Commission that probed the matter. The transcripts of testimony before the commission and its report were useful sources of information about the views of city decision makers in the 1985 crisis.

Closer to home, we would like to thank Sally Dewees for editing early drafts of this book. Finally, we would like to express our deep appreciation for the support of our spouses, Gretchen Van Evera and Scilla Wahrhaftig, who helped us clarify our thoughts and edit this book's many drafts. Special thanks go to the rest of our families, who had to endure our single-mindedness and neglect during the preparation of this book.

PART 1
POWELTON VILLAGE, 1978

1

Introduction

Father Paul Washington recalls seeing Mayor Wilson Goode in church one Sunday in April 1985. The mayor asked him whether he had had any dealings with MOVE recently. Father Washington told him he had not. Mayor Goode responded, "I am going to have to move very carefully and cautiously, because we want to avoid making any of the mistakes that were made back there in 1978 [when a long-brewing conflict with MOVE erupted in a shoot-out in which one policeman was killed]."

A month later, on May 13, 1985, the assault on MOVE's Osage Avenue headquarters began. Police shot 10,000 rounds of ammunition in a 90-minute period from automatic weapons, machine guns, and antitank guns. Finally they dropped a bomb from a helicopter, starting a fire that incinerated five MOVE members and six children. Sixty-one homes lay in smoldering ruins, about 110 houses were damaged, and 250 people were left homeless.

What "mistakes" were Mayor Goode and the city trying to avoid? What urban conflict could require such a violent response? What was MOVE? Why was MOVE's conflict with the city peculiar and different from other group confrontations with the police? What lessons were learned from the 1978 shoot-out that led to the catastrophic response in 1985? Did the city have other avenues for handling this conflict better? Did the response solve the problem, or is it likely to emerge again? Why did this conflict continue to escalate with ever increasing stakes? What lessons can be drawn from this conflict about dealing with similar situations in the future?

These are some of the multitude of questions that arise from the Philadelphia MOVE crisis. This book attempts to answer some of them. At the beginning, we were hesitant about undertaking the research because the case appeared too bizarre, and it seemed unlikely that anything coherent could be learned from it. Our information initially was limited to press accounts and cursory comments from some observers who characterized MOVE as "crazy" or "irrational." Thus, we were concerned whether the conflict lent itself to rational analysis and discussion, and whether it was methodologically possible or valid to analyze irrational behavior rationally. However, despite the methodological problem, the MOVE problem could not be easily dismissed, since many feared that the conflict was not yet over and might emerge with even greater force. We felt there was a need to explore to what extent other conflict-resolution mechanisms could be used to manage this conflict effectively in the future.

An encouraging hint emerged during our research when one close observer we interviewed described MOVE's behavior as "rationally irrational." Once we felt that there might be some rational basis for their "irrationality," our skepticism about the validity of the study began to diminish. As we delved further into the research, we found out that the label "irrational" was misleading because it was used so subjectively. Many used it to refer to views or behavior of somebody they did not understand or, even worse, did not like. Once we were able to go beyond the "rational/irrational" label and recognize the basic premises of MOVE's world view, it was possible to see a consistent, explainable logic in MOVE's behavior. The situation began to resemble a cross-cultural conflict rather than a dispute between a rational party and an irrational party.

Further exploration into the case revealed that the conflict was much more complex than a cursory view might suggest. It was not just one kind of conflict, but many different types overlapping each other. The most visible was the community conflict that revolved around life-style issues. But below the surface we discovered racial, economic, class, philosophical, and political conflicts. Initially, the parties appeared to be the city and MOVE. But a closer examination revealed a multitude of parties and interest groups. In addition, even though the dispute appeared on the surface to be like any other conflict within a society, it took on many of the characteristics of an international conflict. Moreover, during the lifetime of the conflict, almost all forms of conflict containment and resolution techniques were used. These included force (police action), adjudication, negotiation, and mediation.

Thus, we felt that the study would be of value not only to those interested in the MOVE conflict, but also to students of conflict resolution in general. It illustrates the many facets of a complex conflict and the various mechanisms of dealing with it. Among other things it shows the evolution and dynamics of a conflict process. It features many approaches to dispute resolution, the benefits as well as the limitations of each, and the complexity of managing conflicts where the parties have major value and world-view differences.

This book emphasizes negotiation and mediation, though other conflict resolution mechanisms were used as well. We contend that negotiation and mediation are the most viable methods available to contain, if not resolve, this kind of conflict. Adjudication is ineffective particularly if one party does not recognize the rules of the process to be fair and just. The win-lose approach of court litigation seldom addresses the root causes of the conflict. The use of force may not be effective either, since the underlying problems behind the conflict remain unresolved. Coerced solutions usually contain the seeds of future conflict and tension.

Negotiation and bargaining have the potential of reaching the root problems. However, these processes have limited success when they are undertaken without third-party intermediation. Left to their own devices, the parties' modes of communication often heighten the conflict. Their messages may be indirect, discrete, full of threats, warnings, bluffs, and even misinformation. They often become leery of making concessions or compromises for fear of being labeled weak. The range of available alternative solutions is limited by the lack of external sources of information uncolored by the hostilities, stereo-types, suspicions, fears, and prejudices of the conflicting parties.

Third-party intermediary intervention, on the other hand, incorporates many of the benefits of negotiation while rectifying some of its shortcomings. As in negotiation, the parties maintain independence in decision making, participation in the resolution process, and the ability to confront the root causes of their conflict. However, the third party can help translate misunderstood communication, filter distorted messages, encourage open and frank dialogue, expand the range of solutions, and provide face-saving devices for concession and settlement. The intervenor can encourage commitment to the results of the negotiations by creating a forum in which the parties are able to present their cases fairly and justly.[1]

However, mediation in conflicts where at least one of the parties is an extremist poses a special challenge. Extremist groups can be defined as organizations that propound extreme change of the economic, political, or social system.[2] MOVE's public rhetoric, which called for a total transformation of society, could easily earn it the extremist label. While there may have been an incongruity between much of MOVE's rhetoric and its deeds, the value and world view differences between MOVE and its adversaries magnified the perception of extremism and dangerousness. Even though the extreme views that the parties held might not be reconcilable, there remains a strong role for mediation. Mediators can be a vital aid in searching for common ground by translating and interpreting parties' needs and interests in order to focus on finding ways of avoiding violent confrontation and establishing grounds for peaceful coexistence.

It is for these reasons that we emphasize third-party intermediation. We shall examine the various third-party roles undertaken in this case, analyze the factors that contributed to their success or failure, and evaluate their effectiveness in conflicts of this nature.

The book is divided into two parts. The first recounts the period from MOVE's inception to the first major confrontation; the 1978 shoot-out between MOVE and the police. In

Chapter 2 we present how MOVE members described their philosophy and their organization, and how they perceived themselves and the society around them. Whether one agrees with them or not, it is important to understand the premises underlying MOVE's world view in order to understand their behavior and the dynamics of the conflict. Furthermore, since the parties' perceptions and misperceptions played a large role in this conflict, it is important to see the situation from their respective points of view as well as from the outsiders' perspective. While our emphasis is first on MOVE's perception, the later chapters present the other parties' and mediators' views of MOVE. We shall examine how these perceptions determined the parties' responses to each other and the strategies chosen by the intermediaries.

Part 1 continues with Chapter 3, where we trace the evolution of the conflict from a life-style clash with neighbors to one in which the police, courts, and other public officials were involved. We highlight the various perceptions, actions, and counteractions that became turning points in the escalating spiral of the conflict. Then, before discussing the third-party interventions, we summarize in Chapter 4 all the issues, the parties, and their positions, to enable the reader to understand the thrust and rationale of the various conflict resolution efforts.

Chapters 5 and 6 present the various attempts by neighborhood groups, outside individuals, and organizations to negotiate and mediate the conflict. We describe the characteristics of the third parties, the approaches and the processes used, the tactics and strategies applied, and evaluate the effectiveness of the interventions.

Part 2 focuses on the period following the 1978 shoot-out through the 1985 conflagration. It starts, in Chapter 7, with the dispersion and the reappearance of MOVE, and the trials of those MOVE members who were charged in the death of a police officer in the 1978 confrontation. We highlight the perceptions and misperceptions of the parties that determined their tragic strategy choices in waging their conflict.

In Chapter 8, we present the various attempts at negotiation and third-party intervention to avert the 1985 disaster, and we evaluate the efforts. We then examine the post-1985 MOVE-city relationships and prospects of future conflict. We conclude, in Chapter 9, by identifying approaches that could be used in dealing with future tensions with MOVE. We also explore general lessons that could be derived from this experience about conflicts of this nature and the viability of certain conflict resolution mechanisms.

The few works that have been published about the MOVE conflict have not delved into the conflict resolution processes. Therefore, we relied mainly on primary sources, such as interviews, unpublished contemporary documents, and newspaper accounts. Quotations that appear in the text without attribution are derived from interviews we conducted in 1986 and 1987. Quotes from other sources are attributed with appropriate citations.

NOTES

1. Hizkias Assefa, *Mediation of Civil Wars: Approaches and Strategies— The Sudan Conflict* (Boulder, CO: Westview Press, 1987), pp. 7–8.

2. Walter Raymond, *Dictionary of Politics* (Lawrenceville, VA: Brunswick Publishing Co., 1978).

2

Historical Background

MOVE is short for "The Movement," a radical, activist, counterculture organization that arose in Philadelphia. It is unclear when it began; some recall its existence as far back as 1968. John Africa was the founder and philosophical leader of the organization.

John Africa, whose birth name was Vincent Leophart, was a black handyman who did carpentry work for a community housing cooperative in the Powelton Village section of West Philadelphia. In return for his services he was given a small house in the area. Apparently he did not live there but kept his dogs in it. According to Sharon Sims Cox, John Africa's niece and former MOVE member:

People called him the Dog Man. Everywhere he went, he had a trail of dogs behind him. He took care of pets for rich people and used the money to feed the animals fresh meat. He didn't believe in feeding dogs out of a can. He was bent on protecting all life. If he saw a fly struggling in a puddle of water, he'd take the time to get it out so it wouldn't drown. . . . He stayed in a house with candles, because he knew the danger of electricity. He never had any need for technology. He didn't care about clothes or cars or money in his pocket. Any money he got, he gave away.[1]

John Africa is described as a kind and sensitive person who was also very consistent:

Our personalities would fluctuate but he was the same always, consistent in everything—his diet, his strategies, his exercise, his love. He was always very strong and always did physical work. His voice was so deep and powerful, like a roar of thunder. We never felt inhibited around him. He understood us. He made bad seem good. Everybody was naturally drawn to his goodness. You would be mesmerized by him.[2]

Donald Glassey, a white community college professor, resided in Powelton Village. He had been a social work graduate student at the University of Pennsylvania. "Glassey felt strongly about people, especially poor people having a say in the decisions that affect their lives. His master's thesis was 'Citizen Participation and the Poor,' much of it . . . based on his own experience working in New Jersey poverty programs during college summer vacations."[3] Like many in the 1970s, Glassey seemed to be looking for meaning to society and his own life. He said, "I was trying to find out some things. I realized it wasn't happening with different religions. I wasn't any closer to understanding, and so, well, I went on to the next thing." Then he met John Africa, "a short, very friendly black man who walked stray dogs like a Pied Piper. He spoke of his strange philosophy of life. And Glassey listened with fascination."[4] When describing John Africa, Glassey said, "He was the first man I have met who was living in complete harmony with what he believed in."[5] After he met Leophart, Glassey reportedly transcribed Leophart's dictations into an 800-page typescript book, "The Guideline." This book set forth John Africa's teachings and MOVE's philosophy.

Some have described MOVE's philosophy as "urban, back to nature, and primitivist." According to "The Guideline," MOVE stood against everything that is "unnatural" and "man-made." As put by one member,

MOVE's belief is life, natural law. We don't believe in man's reform world system. Life, natural law, which is synonymous with God, made pure air, clean water, fertile soil, made babies healthy and made the principle of freedom, equality for all life without prejudice. This is the law MOVE believes in and obeys, not man's so called laws. It is man's law that has created and sanctioned industry that is polluting the air, poisoning the water, the soil; causing the retarded babies, diseased adults; and lying to the people to cover up this filth. . . . People compromise health and pollution for money and for their life-styles.[6]

MOVE saw its purpose as

. . . stopping man's system from imposing on life . . . stop[ping] industry from poisoning the air, the water, the soil . . . put[ting] an end to enslavement of life—people, animals, any form of life. MOVE's work is to show people how corrupt, rotten, criminally enslaving this system is; [to] show people, through John Africa's teaching, the truth, [and to show] that this system is the cause of all their problems (alcoholism, drug addiction, unemployment, wife abuse, child abuse, child pornography, every problem in the world). People are faced daily with the threat of industrial poison, police brutality, corrupt government, politicians, judges, prisons . . . [MOVE] sets the example of revolution for people to follow. Our work is to confront this system upfront to show people not only that they can fight this system and win, but to show them the urgent need to fight.[7]

MOVE members believed that the city was at the heart of the problem, and that therefore their organization should be based in an urban environment:

As long as the city exists, to move to the country would be to divert from the problem and not to correct it. Diversion is not correction, to divert is to ignore and to ignore a problem is to allow it to grow and fester, get even worse. The city was once the country. But it is city now, because the sickness MOVE is talking about spread itself and will keep spreading if it isn't stopped. It is MOVE's work to stop this sickness.[8]

When the organization was founded, a group of John Africa's friends and relatives used to gather in his house for "study sessions" of "The Guideline." Soon, both black and white people from different backgrounds attended the sessions and joined the organization. For instance, Delbert Africa was a Black Panther member who had fled from Chicago and was working as a youth organizer in a black ghetto in Philadelphia. He met a MOVE member on the street. Delbert reminisced, "He impressed me with the surety of his knowledge and the clarity of the examples he was giving out." About a year later he joined. Delbert said, "The Black Panthers never brought forth the true communist society they preached about. I read the book and saw that you must start with a personal revolution."[9]

Louise James, who became a prominent MOVE spokesperson after the 1985 confrontation, expressed her reasons for joining.

Before I came to the MOVE organization, I am the type of person who has always looked for something that would help me to find justice. I have never liked the injustice, the prejudice, the oppression in this system. However, I have never thought of myself as a leader, but I felt that I could be a good follower. And because I felt that way, I was constantly seeking out people to follow. Prior to MOVE, for example, I followed and supported the Black Panther Party. I followed Angela Davis; I was mesmerized by that woman. I thought she had it all together. I thought she was just brave, courageous and a black woman with a purpose. I felt she had been misused and abused. I followed both George and Johnson Jackson. As I continued to see nothing working in this political system for me, I continued to search. When I came across the teachings of John Africa, my search ended.[10]

About other MOVE members Delbert observed, "We come from all backgrounds of life, college students, ex-prostitutes, businessmen, career women, registered nurses. The thing that drew all of us together was that we were looking for answers. We found it in MOVE and didn't want to take the search any further."

Alberta Africa described the reason people joined the organization:

When MOVE people first joined, we were unhealthy, confused, had all kinds of problems; mental and physical and no solution, just like the people in this system. We were drug addicts, alcoholics, cigarette smokers, thieves, liars. Merle Africa had cancer, Delbert was crippled from a broken back suffered in a car accident, he could barely walk, he was told by doctors that he would never run. Debbie was sterile. Because of John Africa, Merle didn't have cancer no more, Delbert can run as long and as hard as he wants, Debbie and her husband

Source: Bulletin/Temple University Photojournalism Collection

have children. John Africa gave MOVE the solution to all our problems, took us off drugs, cleaned us up in mind and body, made us healthy, strong, correct, gave us the goodness, the wisdom of understanding of life's law.

Other members talked about the changes that took place in their lives after they joined MOVE. Susan Africa, a white member, talked about her upper-middle-class background, and her life as a sickly child, and her recurring bouts of hepatitis as an adolescent. She described her mother and herself as manic depressives. "I am now 31 years, and my health is incredible. I can run 35 miles." She said that she gave birth to her first baby before she joined MOVE. It weighed about six pounds, and her 36-hour labor was very painful. "My second child was born in MOVE, at home with no medical attention. That same day, I ran five miles." Phil Africa talked about his past life as a drug addict and a "stickup man," and how he was able to transform his life after he joined MOVE.

Sharon Sims Cox, an original member, said:

Why did people get involved with MOVE? They were looking for satisfaction. Soon I learned to be satisfied with what I needed not what I wanted. I felt at peace. I became so strong and secure that I could confront the whole world. Let me tell you, we had a helluva lot of good times. The more I hung around, the more MOVE became my life, my existence. I didn't feel inferior anymore. I didn't have to be pushed around and accept things.[11]

All MOVE members adopted Africa as a last name, signifying that they were members of the same family. They grew long hair, which they wore in dreadlocks like the Rastafarians. Some of them started living communally as an extended family. According to Cox, "What attracted me was the warmth and sincerity. It felt good to be with a group of people who were like family. They made me feel like I was somebody."[12]

MOVE's life-style reflected its opposition to modern technology. They sought to avoid using machinery or electricity, cooking food, consuming any kind of processed food, heating houses, or using soap. Their diet was primarily fruits, vegetables, and

nuts. Babies were born the "natural way," at home as prescribed by "The Guideline." They did not refer to "death." Instead, they used the word "cycle" to indicate that life moved to
another form after death.

Marriage and family were strongly encouraged among the
members, and sexual relations outside marriage were prohib-
ited. According to John Africa, MOVE children were to be taught
from "The Guideline" and not in the public schools:

We didn't send our children to school because basically, reading and
writing is what got the system where it is today. Under natural law,
when there were no books or no schools, everybody, more or less,
depended on their natural ability to do things. From education and
reading books, people learn to do things the easy way, without working. From the bike came the car, then the plane, and all those forms
of technology made man weaker and weaker and more dependent on
technology than on himself.[13]

MOVE members did not believe in disposing of their refuse
in the conventional manner. They left most of the remains from
their fruit and vegetable diet in their backyard so that it would
be "cycled" back to nature. They had outhouses.

When the kids, who did not have diapers on, went to the bathroom,
mostly it was outside and we'd dig a hole and cover it like cats do. . . .
We constantly cleaned because we had so many dogs (we kept fifty or
sixty dogs) and children. We washed windows, we mopped and scrubbed
floors every day. We took baths all the time. We just didn't use soap
or deodorant because it is full of chemicals. Strong body odor . . . got
purified from the diet.
    In all the seasons, we tried to keep the children with as little clothes
as possible, we did not bundle them up. Your skin gets weaker from
clothes. You don't put a sweater on your face and my face is stronger
than the rest of my body. We wanted to make their skin tough so their
outside would be as strong as their inside.[14]

MOVE members had a rigorous schedule of physical exercise
that involved the children as well as the dogs. They usually got
up around 4:30 A.M. and took their bus to the park to run and
do calisthenics. The men reportedly ran 10 or 15 miles, wear-

ing knapsacks packed with telephone books or bricks. Every member claimed to be healthy and strong.

To earn their livelihood, MOVE members washed cars on the street across from their headquarters in return for donations. In the winter they shoveled snow for homeowners who were sympathizers. They also sold fruits and vegetables on the street.

Even though their philosophy denounced technology, they tolerated its use by some members.

Every one has to go at his own speed. . . . We do not believe in cooked food. But some guys, their mothers have been feeding them cooked food for 20 years, they just ain't ready to give it up. . . . We don't believe in heating the house—but we recognize we got to. And wood is less high on the technology scale than oil and gas.[15]

Some observers have indicated that part of MOVE's strategy was "to use technology to destroy technology."[16] Therefore, it could use electrically powered bullhorns to spread its message.

Ramona Africa, a MOVE spokesperson, was a law student before she joined. She said that she had attended some of the MOVE trials in the mid-1970s and was repelled by the courts and the police abuse, and became attracted by John Africa's law. When she was interviewed in prison, she summarized MOVE members' dedication to their beliefs:

We are bound to MOVE law, to our religion, to John Africa by the love John Africa gives us. This is the difference between John Africa and this system. This system tries to bind people to the system through intimidation instead of love. Nobody accepts intimidation, but everybody accepts love. People want to free themselves from intimidation . . . but nobody wants to free themselves of love. This is why I know I ain't crazy to leave the security and love I get from the Coordinator [John Africa] for the insecurity and dissatisfaction of this system. MOVE people refuse to compromise our religion in spite of the ungodly intimidation spewed on us by this system. We are sometimes labeled fanatics, but we are not fanatics any more than Christians were for remaining loyal to their beliefs despite the ungodly intimidation they suffered under the Roman government.[17]

Ramona testified to the absoluteness of her dedication to MOVE principles at her trial following the May 13, 1985, bombing of MOVE's Osage Avenue residence and the death of 11 adult and children members:

MOVE has constantly been asked, was May 13th worth it? All I can say is it is never worth it to do wrong. If I am doing what is right, then there is nothing else. What else can I do, submit to wrong? You know, what purpose would I have for living at the point that I submit to wrong?

There is no reliable record of how many people were MOVE members. Some newspapers speculated there were about 57 active members and 50 supporters in the late 1970s.[18] However small it may have been, MOVE was poised to have a major impact on the City of Brotherly Love. The stage was set for a series of cataclysmic clashes between the emerging activist counterculture group and the city of Philadelphia. In less than 10 years, these confrontations would claim at least 12 lives, disrupt 2 neighborhoods, paralyze the city, ruin political careers, and send many to prison.

NOTES

1. Sharon Sims Cox, as told to Carol Saline, "My Life in MOVE," *Philadelphia Magazine*, Sept. 1985, p. 169.

2. Ibid.

3. "The Making of a Mover," *Philadelphia Daily News*, Mar. 9, 1978, p. 26.

4. Ibid.

5. Murray Dubin, "Revolution Ain't Verbalized . . . ," *Philadelphia Inquirer*, May 9, 1980, p. A14.

6. MOVE Women, untitled document beginning, "Since the May 13th bombing . . . ," apparently written by MOVE women imprisoned in State Correctional Institute, Muncy, PA, 1986 (?).

7. Ibid.

8. Ibid.

9. "MOVE Considers Glassey a Judas," *Philadelphia Daily News*, Mar. 10, 1978, p. 8.

10. Transcript of testimony before the Philadelphia Special Inves-

tigation Commission, *Philadelphia Inquirer*, Oct. 28, 1985, special section.

   11. Cox, "My Life in MOVE," p. 171.

   12. Ibid., p. 170.

   13. Ibid., p. 171.

   14. Ibid., p. 172.

   15. Jim Quinn, "The Heart of Darkness," *Philadelphia Magazine* 69, no. 5 (May 1978): 240.

   16. Kitty Caparella, "Will MOVE Rise Again?" *Philadelphia Daily News*, Mar. 24, 1986, p. 19.

   17. MOVE Women, "Since the May 13 Bombing. . . . "

   18. Caparella, "Will MOVE Rise Again?" p. 19.

3

The Evolution of the Conflict

THE SOCIAL AND POLITICAL CONTEXT

MOVE evolved in the socially and politically polarized climate of the early 1970s. It was the Nixon and Watergate era. A great deal of social unrest surrounded the civil rights movement, Vietnam, and Cambodia. Radical groups, such as the Black Panthers and the Symbionese Liberation Army, were either active or fresh in people's minds. During this time in Philadelphia, Frank Rizzo, a former police commissioner, became mayor. He projected himself as a tough "law and order" politician. During his administration blacks and liberals accused the police of systematic civil rights abuses. Police had no firearms policy to limit individual officers' discretion on the appropriate use of weapons. The district attorney's office was said to be so involved in investigating killings by law enforcement that it was not able to handle complaints of police brutality.

The community where MOVE began to operate, Powelton Village, was a racially integrated neighborhood that included students, university teachers, New Left groups, and collectives, and was a center of a variety of organizing activities. It was located near a semighetto neighborhood and had two expanding universities, Drexel Institute of Technology and the University of Pennsylvania, for neighbors. Community members were concerned that poor blacks were being pushed out of the area by university expansion and gentrification development. It was against this background that the conflict evolved between MOVE, its neighbors, and later the city.

LIFE-STYLE CONFLICT

In 1973, Donald Glassey, an original white MOVE member, bought a house on 3rd Street in Powelton Village and invited other MOVE members to move in. There they established a headquarters, and about five of the members began to live there communally according to their back-to-nature beliefs. Others resided in nearby apartments and in other parts of the city.

MOVE's life-style began to bring them into conflict with their Powelton neighbors. People complained about garbage and fecal odor, rat infestation, and health and housing code violations. They were concerned about the health hazard from the many unvaccinated dogs that MOVE kept in its house. Also, MOVE's practice of not sending their children to school and dressing them minimally, even in the winter, raised neighbors' concerns about child neglect. Some neighbors made their grievances known directly to MOVE; others complained to city officials and the police.

MOVE responded by pointing out how the neighbors' way of living offended them equally. "People complained about our life-style, but their life-style was just as awful to us," complained Phil Africa. Another member, Susan Cox, recalled:

They [the neighbors] would smoke marijuana about half the night. They would snort cocaine. They would play loud, loud music. They would fight. MOVE never went to the city officials or policemen to make complaints. But when MOVE practiced our religion by letting orange peels cycle in the dirt, they complained about us. It was really unfair.[1]

Phil Africa contended that even if MOVE created the odor, the smell it produced was less dangerous to life than the smell of industrial pollution. Polluted air affected everybody, including MOVE members. Thus, MOVE felt the neighbors were in no position to dictate to it about life-styles.

Concerning the rat infestation complaints, MOVE responded:

They [the neighbors are] making a big fuss over the rats, but the rats were there before we got to the area. We would put food out for our dogs and to feed the birds, so the rats came into our backyard from the rest of the neighborhood. I guess they felt they would get a better meal with us because we leave our apple, banana, and sweet potato peels on top of the ground to be recycled. To us rats were just animals trying to survive like any thing else. Because life is important to us we didn't want to starve them. As long as they ate good, they never bothered us.[2]

Neither side convinced the other, and the neighborhood conflict grew. Rhetoric intensified. The neighbors who actively protested against MOVE complained that MOVE retaliated by threatening and harassing them, picketing their houses, and shouting obscenities at them over loudspeakers. For instance, when MOVE applied for a dog kennel permit, a group of neighborhood residents appeared at a zoning board hearing to oppose them. Afterward they complained that MOVE members verbally harassed them and threatened them with "castration." One elderly neighbor died of a heart attack that some people attributed to MOVE's threats.

By the mid-1970s MOVE members began appearing at public functions. They received public notice when they demonstrated against the Philadelphia Zoo for caging animals. They disrupted rallies, conferences, Board of Education meetings, and neighborhood block parties throughout West Philadelphia. They used these events as platforms to propagate MOVE's views on education and "the system." Delbert and Jerry Africa formed a group called the "flying squad" for this purpose. They drowned out speakers by using bullhorns to read excerpts from the MOVE book. Their language was littered with profanities. When people criticized them for their obscenities, their reply was "Those words were here before we got here. What is profane is the megaton bomb and the guns the police wear on their hips. Profanity is rape and cops beating on people with blackjacks"[3] or "If our profanity offends you, look around and see how destructively society is profaning itself. It is the rape of the land, it is pollution of the environment that is real obscenity."[4]

Their confrontation with the neighbors and their demonstrations at the zoo, pet shops, circuses, and public functions resulted in clashes with police. They were frequently arrested and jailed for disorderly conduct, failure to disperse, obstruction of justice, and resisting arrest. MOVE members complained that they were beaten. When some were arrested, the remaining members would "go over to a police district where our brothers were locked up, and carry signs to get the police to let them go. We didn't attack people; we attacked their ways. The more we were being jailed, the more we demonstrated." These demonstrations, in turn, led to further arrests, clashes with the police, and beatings.

In this period police brutality and abuse of rights was a major issue in Philadelphia's black community. In 1974 MOVE started to focus on these issues and speak about them. They began to garner support because they championed a major grievance of the black community. This focus led to even more confrontations with police. According to one account, in a 7-month period in 1975, MOVE members had been arrested on misdemeanor charges more than 150 times, fined $15,000, and sentenced to several years in jail.[5]

Police efforts to implement the city's orders became a source of another series of clashes. For instance, one of MOVE's primary income sources was washing cars. They performed this service on the street. As their car wash grew popular, neighbors complained of traffic congestion and excess water and mud in the streets. The city responded to the grievances by deciding to close the car wash for failure to obtain a license. When police came to enforce this decision, Glassey complained, "The police closed down the car wash even though we had permission from the courts."[6]

When MOVE members were brought in for their trials, they refused to show respect to the courts. They saw courts as extensions of the system they were fighting against. The judicial system administered what MOVE called "human law," instead of the "law of nature." To them, man's law was the source of all the evil in society. When they were brought to trial, they refused to be respresented by lawyers, as they believed that no lawyer understood them. No one could represent them earnestly. Thus, they acted as their own defense counsel. Their seemingly outrageous and flamboyant style of presenting their case not only masked their message but also brought the wrath of the courts on them.

MOVE also used the trials to publicize John Africa's teachings. They often responded to questions with long monologues. They refused to swear to tell the truth because their only truth was John Africa's, and they would tell only John Africa's truth. Judges found this behavior to be outrageous and responded by giving them steep contempt sentences. Sue Africa remarked, "[Since MOVE started] we MOVE members have been arrested more than six hundred times, bail totalling more than one million dollars, and fifty years total in contempt charges, and vicious beatings of those that are arrested."[7] "And, honestly," added Phil Africa, "we have never done anything criminal. We just want to be left alone."[8] In MOVE's perception, it was being harassed and imprisoned for its political and religious beliefs.

A TURNING POINT

A March 1976 melee with the police became a turning point in the conflict. Some MOVE members held a spontaneous party for a group of their colleagues who had just been released from jail. Soon a fight broke out between MOVE and the police. MOVE and police accounts of the conflict differ. Police said that they came at four in the afternoon in response to neighbors' calls complaining about noise. As they tried to disperse the crowd, they were taunted and hit by thrown bricks.[9] Phil Africa said that they were followed from prison by a group of plainclothes police and were attacked when they reached their headquarters.

Several police officers and MOVE members suffered injuries. This resulted in charges being filed against three MOVE leaders; Jerry, Conrad, and Robert Africa, for aggravated assault on police officers. The charges were the most serious to be lodged against MOVE up to that point.

MOVE complained that a six-week-old baby, Life Africa, was

killed during this incident. Phil Africa, the baby's father, re-counted, "My wife was holding my son. She was trying to stay in front to keep the cops from getting the men. They just knocked her down: stomped her and the baby." Police denied the charge, saying that no baby was involved in the conflict. MOVE was asked to present a birth certificate to prove that a baby really existed. However, since MOVE believed in home birth and not registering their children, they were unable to present a birth certificate. According to one account:

Police [were] checking out the report late yesterday, but tended to discount the allegation. "We are skeptical of the story, said a high ranking police official. The baby was not born in a hospital and there is no record of birth."[10]

Instead, MOVE offered witnesses to testify that there was a baby, but that approach was rejected by the authorities. The police asked MOVE to present the body for an autopsy, but MOVE refused because autopsies violated its philosophy. MOVE next invited some newspeople and a black member of the City Council to its headquarters to show them the body. Meanwhile, MOVE's complaint was dismissed for lack of evidence. This, in turn, reinforced MOVE's perception that the system was totally unjust and was determined to exterminate it.

One of those invited to the viewing at the MOVE house was City Councilman Lucien Blackwell. He later commented, "I found that the way they looked from the street was entirely different from the way that they lived. I found that the day that I arrived. We went inside, everything was clean."[11]

Six months later, MOVE members displayed the body of an-other infant. They complained that this one was stillborn with a fractured head resulting from a police beating of a pregnant MOVE member. At this point, John Africa altered his nonvi-olent stance and took the position that MOVE would counter with violence if attacked. Ramona Africa clarified this position by saying that nonviolence is not synonymous with masochism. Self-defense is God's law. She also commented that Martin Lu-ther King's version of nonviolence encourages violence. It en-courages people to continue hitting you.

MOVE Protesters Claiming a Baby Was Killed by Police

Source: Bulletin/Temple University Photojournalism Collection

Although charges against the police in the March 1976 melee were dropped, three MOVE leaders were accused of assault and related crimes. Joel Todd, a young white lawyer who would later play an intermediary role, was appointed to serve as Jerry Africa's backup attorney, since MOVE would not allow an attorney to represent them directly. The three leaders were convicted and sentenced to prison, becoming the first MOVE members to be given long sentences in state prison. MOVE interpreted the convictions as a political decision to exterminate their organization and silence the members. They called the three leaders political prisoners and began demanding their release. Freeing its prisoners became MOVE's major focus.

Meanwhile, another branch of the city took action. In response to the neighbors' complaints, the Department of Licenses and Inspection had unsuccessfully tried to enter MOVE's house to check for compliance with health and building codes. Finally, in July 1976, the city announced plans for an inspection of the MOVE house by police, health officials, and social workers. The latter were to inspect the condition of the children in the MOVE house. MOVE refused to allow entry, stating, "Any inspection violates the sanctity of our home, and we will consider any incursion as a declaration of war." They built an eight-foot wall to keep the inspectors out.[12]

According to the *Philadelphia Daily News*, by early May 1977, John Africa was "telling followers a police raid on MOVE was imminent, and fear of police brutality was heightened because of published accusations in a *Philadelphia Inquirer* series [which reported on a four-month investigation into police brutality]."[13] On May 20, 1977, a MOVE member was evicted from a nearby apartment, a scuffle ensued, and he was arrested. MOVE members appeared on the porch of their barricaded headquarters, wearing uniforms and carrying guns for the first time. Neighbors saw the weapons and called the police. Tensions heightened when one MOVE member was arrested on the street for carrying a gun. More than 200 police were sent to the MOVE headquarters. Stakeout officers with high-powered rifles took positions in nearby apartment buildings, while other police cleared the streets. The confrontation lasted about nine hours, but was defused without violence. However, authorities charged 11 MOVE members with weapons violations. The city vowed to maintain a massive police presence to arrest the MOVE members on these charges when they stepped outside their headquarters. About 100 plainclothes police were deployed around the clock in the area. The siege of MOVE headquarters had begun.

On July 21, 1977, federal agents seized numerous explosives, chemicals used to make explosives, and firearms during a raid on a house that belonged to a MOVE member. Donald Glassey, an original MOVE member, had turned police informant and led the FBI to the arms cache. He implicated MOVE "in a bizarre bomb plot which involved setting up explosive devices in hotels and embassies around the country and in London."[14] According to a handwritten letter reportedly handed to police by MOVE, MOVE warned the city:

Don't attempt to enter MOVE headquarters or harm MOVE people unless you want an international incident. . . . We are prepared to hit reservoirs, empty hotels and apartment houses, close factories and tie up traffic in major cities of Europe. . . . We want Robert Africa, Gerald Africa and Conrad Africa released from Grateford Prison and flown by helicopter to MOVE headquarters immediately. . . . We are not going to negotiate with you unless you release our people. . . .[15]

In the end, six MOVE members, including John Africa in absentia, were convicted of conspiracy to violate federal weapons and explosives laws. (Eventually, on July 22, 1981, John and Alphonso Africa were acquitted of the charges.)[16]

The siege continued for about ten months and cost the city $1.2 million.[17] During the siege, MOVE supporters and other sympathetic groups brought food and supplies through police lines to sustain MOVE. It became a stalemate. The prolonged police presence was not only expensive and disruptive, it was not achieving its goal of pressuring MOVE to get out of its headquarters. In fact, it generated more support for MOVE. The city then obtained an order from Judge Fred DiBona to set up a full blockade. They sought to cut off utilities and prevent the entry of food, water, and other necessities. The stated purpose was to starve out the occupants of the house and arrest them when they came out.

A Quiet Sunday Morning in Powelton (MOVE Headquarters)

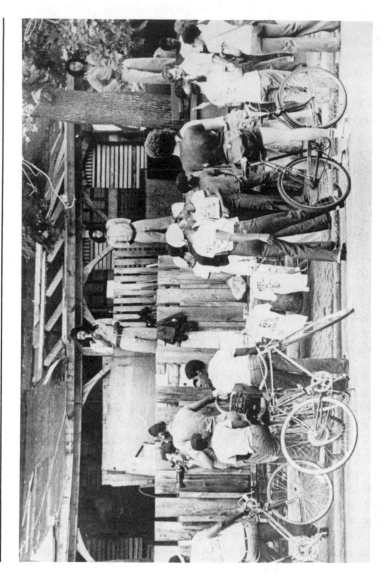

NEIGHBORS AGAINST NEIGHBORS

As the conflict between MOVE and the police escalated, and preparations for the blockade were under way, neighborhood groups in Powelton began to argue with each other over how to handle their problems with MOVE and to what extent the police should be involved. The massive police presence heightened the debate. The *Philadelphia Tribune* reported that "As the MOVE-police conflict stalemates . . . the battle has now shifted to neighborhood community groups."[18]

One group of neighbors formed the Powelton Emergency Human Rights Committee (PEHRC). They took the position that MOVE's behavior was making the neighborhood uninhabitable. Some of them were concerned about declining property values, since the unsanitary and unsightly condition of MOVE's compound was driving people away. They sought to involve the police and the city to evict MOVE. One PEHRC member served as their attorney. He also owned the other half of the building that had become MOVE's headquarters.

PEHRC brought a federal civil rights suit against MOVE. The city agreed to help with the suit. PEHRC explained its motivation in a telegram to the press.

The suit is prompted by MOVE threats of beatings, mutilation, and death directed against community residents opposing MOVE's uninoculated dogs, deliberate breeding of rats, and possession of illegal guns. PEHRC also asked Mayor Rizzo to maintain police protection for the community, demanding prompt nonviolent action to end MOVE's threat and criminal activities.[19]

In 1978, when the city's decision to blockade MOVE was appealed to the Pennsylvania Supreme Court, PEHRC filed a brief supporting the city's position: "PEHRC joins with the City of Philadelphia in requesting that a blockade be immediately set up surrounding the perimeter of MOVE headquarters in a manner to be determined by the City of Philadelphia and its police department."[20]

Another group of neighbors was formed called Powelton United Neighbors (PUN). It seriously opposed police and city

Source: Bulletin/Temple University Photojournalism Collection

intervention, and became particularly concerned about the siege and the preparation for the blockade. It described itself as a group of residents working for a peaceful resolution to the crisis. Peaceful coexistence with MOVE was possible, they felt, and their problem could be handled through negotiation instead of police intervention. "We believe that any problems the community has with MOVE should be solved by the community and that the police cannot help us."[21]

PUN held press conferences at which they pointed out that the mass police presence in the neighborhood was making an already tense atmosphere worse. It was escalating the potential for a violent confrontation in which many people, including neighbors, MOVE, and police, could be hurt or killed. They presented a petition demanding the blockade be dismantled and police be withdrawn, since "The underlying problems between MOVE and other Powelton residents cannot be resolved by police action." They stated that they would

. . . oppose a police raid or starve out of MOVE and police harassment of our neighbors. We do this not out of support for MOVE's religion, politics or actions but because the threats, rats and garbage, though they wrongfully infringe on the right of others, do not justify starvation or massacre of MOVE members and because the aftermath of such a course would be polarization, heightened racial tensions, widespread fear and danger, and the probable destruction of the best features of Powelton as a community.

We are an interracial community. United action by black and white residents has been at the heart of the success of our community.[22]

One PUN member summed up the organization's basic position thus:

Don't get me wrong . . . we have had a lot of problems with MOVE in the neighborhood. Last summer we talked to them about the garbage they were dumping in their yard and finally got them to compost it. We weren't friends of MOVE, we don't condone everything they did. But we didn't think the police should move in and repress them like they have. We always felt that they were more reasonable and flexible than most people gave them credit for.[23]

PUN presented a petition to the mayor and other city officials pointing out that the police siege was dividing the community along racial lines by prohibiting black people from entering areas near the MOVE headquarters while allowing whites through. They demanded the police be withdrawn and the blockade dismantled.[24] They also organized demonstrations to pressure the mayor to disengage the forces.

The divergent views on how the MOVE conflict should be handled continued to divide the neighborhood. PUN referred to PEHRC as "hardline anti-MOVE with a 'Hatfield & McCoy' vendetta that has festered for years."[25] PEHRC called PUN a group of bleeding-heart liberals who were "interested in the civil rights of MOVE members. But they don't seem to be interested at all in the rights of people who have been threatened by MOVE." The two groups carried their conflict to court. When the court granted the city's blockade petition, which was supported by PEHRC, PUN appealed to the state Supreme Court.

Though these two groups were the most vocal protagonists, other groups were also formed that had a variety of responses to the MOVE crisis. The Powelton Civic Homeowners' Association demanded that the city correct the health, safety, and zoning violations at the MOVE headquarters, and endorsed the use of a third-party mediator to seek a nonviolent end to the state of siege.

The Concerned Citizens to Ensure Justice for MOVE, a predominately black group, took a strong pro-MOVE position. They organized demonstrations to publicize MOVE's concerns. One of their leaflets described MOVE as

. . . breaking the way for oppressed people everywhere. The community has been invaded by the police as a result of a confrontation between the police and MOVE, an organization defending itself against the police. MOVE has been fighting extermination for the past five years. . . . We support MOVE's right to life, freedom, and free speech, and demand an end to their harassment as well as our own.[26]

The Concerned Citizens accused PEHRC of

. . . [writing] a leaflet telling their view of the situation. Their leaflet contains many lies and misstatements. . . . No Philadelphia citizen has even been threatened with a gun by a MOVE member, not even the police. The only thing they have said was "no longer will we be beaten, killed, or intimidated by the police without a like response."[27]

The Concerned Citizens also complained that their own members had been harassed by police since the confrontation between MOVE and the police started.

Another group, Poweltonians for Democratic Action, opposed police involvement. They stated:

We demand community control of police, not police control of our community. If there is a very severe health problem within our community as a result of the rats from MOVE headquarters, what we want is hundreds of cats not hundreds of cops. Cats kill rats, cops kill people. We do not intend to stand around and allow people to be killed, no matter what the method.[28]

Another group, calling itself the African Peoples' Cadre Organization, declared:

Frank Rizzo, the self-proclaimed racist Mayor of Philadelphia seeks to use the starvation death of innocent black men, women, and children to further the sinister aims of his national white supremacy campaign. . . . Therefore, we are here today to bring food and water to our thirsty and starving brothers, sisters, and children.

Meanwhile, another organization, the Tuesday Night Group, was trying to bridge the gaps among the neighborhood factions. It tried to serve as "a clearing house of information and viewpoints . . . and to identify areas of consensus."[29] It took a position demanding that police not raid MOVE, and that police stop harassing people visiting MOVE. "Further," they stated, "we believe it is important for us to talk with MOVE with the hope that we can negotiate our differences with them."[30] A founding member of the Tuesday Night Group said, "One of the really strange things about MOVE and the neighborhood is that not many people have actually gone and talked to MOVE. I went and talked to them, with thirty or forty police watching, and I got a different perspective. I found them fairly reasonable."[31]

The conflict between the neighborhood groups was taking place in a context in which Powelton Village as a whole viewed itself as being in conflict with the Rizzo administration. Powelton residents felt the mayor had ignored them because it was a New Left, racially integrated neighborhood that was overwhelmingly anti-Rizzo.

Many people in PEHRC believe that the reason MOVE was allowed to go on so long is that Frank Rizzo doesn't care at all about Powelton. He's never carried the ward. He knows he'll never carry the ward. He sees people who were demonstrating against him and doesn't much care if they get threatened by a group demonstrating against them.[32]

PUN members also had their share of complaints against the city and the mayor:

In addition to our belief that the police presence is detrimental to the community, we also believe that you, the city and state governments, have not demonstrated any real concern for the problems of this community or the safety and well being of its residents. You have not helped to stop the expansion of Drexel and Penn [both neighboring universities] into this community.

The Redevelopment Authority has paved the way by destroying many available homes, evicting the residents (who are largely poor and black) and condemning the buildings to permit further university expansion. . . . The Community Food Coop, which provided low cost food for residents of Powelton-Mantua [a neighboring black ghetto], was forced to close and the promises of a new building never materialized. You have never provided us with adequate garbage collection or spent the necessary money on exterminating rats.

If MOVE had been located in Chestnut Hill [an affluent white residential neighborhood], the garbage and rats would have been taken care of at the first neighbor's complaint.

Your past record makes us conclude that you have neither the means nor the desire to resolve our problems, including our differences with MOVE, in a manner that would benefit the entire Powelton community.[33]

Powelton residents had been active in combating police abuse. Among neighborhood residents were the attorneys who represented many blacks in civil rights suits against the city and the police. At least some in PUN and the black groups saw the city's treatment of the MOVE case as an extension of the prejudice of the mayor and the police. They charged that the mayor's handling of the issues "remind[s] us too clearly of Rizzo's history of using racism for political ends."[34] They called the police blockade of MOVE's headquarters a "racist assault given the background of Rizzo."[35]

TOWARD THE 1978 SHOOT-OUT

While the conflict between the neighbors was going on, the Supreme Court of Pennsylvania accepted a petition filed by PUN to stay Judge DiBona's decision to impose a full blockade. Justice Robert N. C. Nix, Jr., granted a two-week stay, until the case could be reviewed by the full court. However, after the stay expired, on March 16, 1978, the full court approved the blockade. About 1,000 police sealed off a four-block area with sandbags and snow fencing to ensure that no food, water, or other provisions would reach MOVE. All utilities were disconnected.

Many neighbors and other Philadelphia residents reacted angrily. Some neighbors and black groups threatened to crash the barricades or bring helicopters to drop food for MOVE. Others tried civil disobedience tactics to deliver food. Jim Quinn provides an account of one such effort by a lady from Chestnut Hill, a wealthy white Philadelphia neighborhood.

I met [Mrs. Spaeth] walking down towards the barricade—or rather not walking—she is resting two enormous bags of food on a stone fence, obviously not able to carry them farther. . . .

"I am taking them to the barricade," she says. "I just don't believe we can sit by and watch people starve." Her voice is trembling slightly, her face intent. I try to convince her that there is no way she can get through the barricade. She says she must go down no matter what.

"At least," I say, "give me the bag with a small potted geranium plant sticking out of the top. I will keep it safe for you." "No," she says, "it is to disguise the fact that there is a gallon of water in the bag."

I walk with her the first hundred yards and then watch her go on

MOVE Member Reads Rizzo's Ultimatum

Source: Bulletin/Temple University Photojournalism Collection

alone, obviously just as frightened as she is determined. I wait 'till the cops stop her at the barricade.

"What you are doing is against the law, ma'am," says the polite black plainclothesman . . . "I can't let you pass."

"I am sorry," says the gentle voice of Mrs. Spaeth, "I know it against the law of Philadelphia. But I believe that there is a higher law. As human beings we are not allowed to watch people starve. Or see babies die for lack of water."

She is arrested. . . . Several people, some of them police, are obviously moved. . . . Four or five people a week like Mrs. Spaeth are arrested. . . . [36]

The blockade sparked a series of major interventions to stave off disaster. On May 5, 1978, after two months of mediation, some intermediaries managed to get MOVE and the city to sign an agreement that ended the siege. However, by August 2 the agreement had collapsed, and events started to escalate ending up in a major shoot-out between MOVE and the police. The result was one death, several woundings, and deepened distrust that would lead to worse violence in the future. To understand what went wrong, one must carefully reconstruct the events.

NOTES

1. Sharon Sims Cox, as told to Carol Saline, "My Life in MOVE," *Philadelphia Magazine*, Sept. 1985, p. 238.

2. Ibid., p. 239.

3. Ibid.

4. Murray Dubin, "Revolution Ain't Verbalized . . . ," *Philadelphia Inquirer*, May 9, 1980, p. 14A.

5. Mike Leary, "At the Barricades: Relief, Jubilation," *Philadelphia Inquirer*, May 5, 1978, p. 6A.

6. Kitty Caparella, "True Believer Can't Believe This," *Philadelphia Daily News*, Mar. 10, 1978, p. 8.

7. "Rain Soaks MOVE Rally," *Philadelphia Inquirer*, Mar. 9, 1978, p. 3.

8. Gerald Etter, "Blockade of MOVE off Again," *Philadelphia Inquirer*, Mar. 9, 1978, p. A1.

9. Robert J. Terry, "W. Phila Commune Members Clash with Police: 6 Held," *Philadelphia Inquirer*, Mar. 29, 1976, p. B1.

10. Ibid.

11. "Bombing on Osage Avenue," WHYY TV, 1987. (Transcribed by the authors.)

12. Dubin, "Revolution Ain't Verbalized . . . ," p. 14A.

13. Kitty Caparella, "Bomb Plot Mushrooms into Siege," *Philadelphia Daily News*, Mar. 7, 1978, p. 4.

14. Jim Quinn, "The Heart of Darkness," *Philadelphia Magazine* 69, no. 5 (May 1978): 245.

15. Caparella, "Bomb Plot Mushrooms . . . ," p. 30.

16. "Halting the Cult: A 10 Year Battle," *Philadelphia Daily News*, May 13, 1985, p. 7.

17. Ibid.

18. Linn Washington, "Civil Rights Suit Is Filed Against MOVE," *Philadelphia Daily Tribune*, July 2, 1977, p. 27.

19. PEHRC, telegram to *Philadelphia Daily Tribune*, June 29, 1977.

20. Robert Guzzardi, petition to appear as amicus curiae. Case is cited on appeal as *Philadelphia v. Glassey*, 477P.456, 1977.

21. PUN, petition signed by 150 Powelton residents, delivered to Mayor Rizzo, July 2, 1977. (Mimeographed.)

22. PUN, "Statement: Report of the Powelton United Neighbors," July 19, 1977. (Mimeographed.)

23. Mike Leary, "At the Barricades."

24. PUN, petition.

25. Washington, "Civil Rights Suit," p. 27.

26. Tuesday Night Group, "Fact Sheets on MOVE: What Powelton Neighbors Are Saying," no. 1 (July 8, 1977). (Mimeographed.)

27. Community in Support of MOVE, "An Open Letter to Mayor Rizzo, Our Philadelphia Neighbors and the PEHRC." July 3, 1977. (Mimeographed.)

28. Poweltonians for Democratic Action, press release, June 23, 1977. (Mimeographed.)

29. Tuesday Night Group, "Fact Sheet."

30. Ibid.

31. Washington, "Civil Rights Suit," p. 27.

32. Quinn, "Heart of Darkness," p. 248.

33. PUN, petition.

34. PUN, "Statement."

35. Ibid.

36. Quinn, "Heart of Darkness," p. 252.

4

The Parties and the Issues

Before discussing the various resolution attempts in this complex conflict, it will be helpful to clearly identify all the parties involved and summarize their respective perceptions and positions.

MOVE VS. POWELTON NEIGHBORS

The major issues that generated conflict between the Powelton neighbors and MOVE were the following:

—MOVE's life-style, in particular the smell, the animals, pests, and MOVE's treatment of its children, was offensive to Powelton neighbors. The neighbors tried to bring in the police and the city to get relief.

—MOVE objected to its neighbors' life-style and sought to set an example by living according to "nature's law."

—Some neighbors were concerned about declining property values, since the unsanitary and unsightly condition of MOVE's compound was driving residents away.

—MOVE disrupted neighborhood meetings and activities, such as block parties and political or religious meetings.

—MOVE threatened and harassed those who opposed them in the community or those who complained against them.

Even though these issues were concerns to most Powelton neighbors, they did not speak with one voice. A division arose within the neighborhood over how MOVE should be handled.

PUN VS. PEHRC

—The Powelton United Neighbors (PUN) believed that peaceful co-existence with MOVE was possible and that their problems could be solved through negotiation.

—The Powelton Emergency Human Rights Committee (PEHRC) believed that the problems with MOVE were beyond what the neighborhood could handle, and that city, even police, intervention was necessary.

—The two groups presented opposing briefs in the Supreme Court when the issue of erecting the full blockade of MOVE was considered.

—Local black groups were allied with MOVE, since MOVE championed a major community issue: police abuse.

—There were unsuccessful attempts within the neighborhood to heal the PUN-PEHRC rift. The Tuesday Night Group tried to bring all neighborhood factions together to share concerns and agendas. However, the differences between the groups were not resolved.

While life-style issues were important to the neighborhood groups early in the conflict, they became transformed as the dispute progressed. The massive police deployment created an alliance between former antagonists, PUN and MOVE. The issue of police presence in the community and the impact it had on the neighborhood became paramount, and life-style conflicts faded into the background.

The focus of neighborhood conflict-resolution activities shifted. Rather than focus on their life-style conflicts with MOVE, the neighbors spent their time and energy debating the role of the police. In fact, PUN and the Tuesday Night Group began to function as third parties in the dispute between MOVE and the city. They even filed petitions suggesting possible formulas for resolving that conflict.

MOVE VS. THE CITY

Ordinarily one would view the city as an integrated entity. However, in this conflict, the various organs of government seem to have developed their own vested interests and grievances. It would thus be misleading to treat the city as a monolithic whole. There were at least four subparties within the city with separate interests.

MOVE vs. the Mayor and His Administration

—Mayor Rizzo was seen as a racist law-and-order politician. Some intervenors suggested that Rizzo "hated MOVE's guts."

—MOVE opposed Rizzo and would "try to do anything to expose his racism."

—MOVE could not get a license for its car washing service.

—The Department of Licenses and Inspection had various confrontations with MOVE over health and sanitation violations.

—The city was prosecuting charges against MOVE members arising from MOVE/police confrontations.

—MOVE perceived the Rizzo administration as giving implicit approval to police abuse by not taking action against police officers who beat MOVE members.

—MOVE saw the administration as being primarily interested in evicting it from Powelton Village.

—The Rizzo administration saw MOVE as a troublesome revolutionary group that was developing into a political embarrassment.

MOVE vs. the Police

—MOVE saw its members as being harassed and beaten by police. MOVE became a champion of black grievances against police brutality and repeatedly confronted police, which resulted in more police harassment.

—Intervenors described two factions within the police department. The Civil Affairs Division, headed by Inspector George Fencl, was a highly professional, disciplined unit trained to handle civil disturbances. They talked freely with people involved in confrontations. Some noted that in one year in the tumultuous 1960s, the unit managed to do its job without making a single arrest. The other faction, the regular police, was referred to in terms such as "Rizzo's thugs." Allegations of racism, brutality, and unnecessary killings were generally applied to these regular police units.

—Police who were trying to enforce the judges' and district attorney's orders came into direct confrontation with MOVE.

—Some observers saw the characteristics of gang warfare in the conflict between the police and MOVE: an automatic intolerance for each other and an inclination to clash at every opportune moment.

MOVE vs. the District Attorney's Office

The district attorney is an independently elected public official structurally separate from the city administration. However, he was linked to the MOVE situation, for it was the district attorney's office that prosecuted criminal cases filed by the city police, including those against MOVE members. It also prosecuted citizen complaints against the police. However, MOVE members felt that the district attorney unjustifiably pursued criminal charges against them while ignoring their complaints against the police.

MOVE vs. the Courts

—MOVE ridiculed the court process by refusing to answer questions and lecturing the court that the only true law was John Africa's law. The judges felt that their honor and that of the courts was at stake.

—MOVE used its trials as a platform to publicize its philosophy.

—Judges retaliated by giving MOVE steep contempt sentences.

—MOVE viewed Judge DiBona and others as pro-Rizzo.

—Since MOVE members lacked confidence in the courts, they did not appeal some of the judges' sentences or orders. Joel Todd, who had served as an attorney for one of their leaders, stated, "They [MOVE] did not have much faith in the court system. They felt there was no reason to go further and they didn't think an appeal would gain anything."

—After the shoot-out in August 1978, the judge executed warrants against MOVE members, even those who were not in MOVE's headquarters or were out of state, on charges that had been held in abeyance by the agreement.[1]

—Nine MOVE members were sentenced to 30-100 years, and another to 20-30 years, on charges arising out of the death of the policeman in the shoot-out.

THE NEIGHBORHOOD VS. THE MAYOR

—Powelton villagers felt the mayor had ignored their community because it was overwhelmingly anti-Rizzo. They accused the city of not providing the services it made available to other sections of the city.

—Many in the neighborhood were involved in efforts to curb police abuses. They saw the city's handling of the MOVE case as an extension of the prejudice of the mayor and the police.

NOTE

1. "MOVE Blockade on Again," *The Evening Tribune*, Mar. 8, 1978, p. 1.

5

Third-Party Intervention: Early Period

Many people offered their services as intermediaries in this complex conflict. Those interventions before the 1978 shoot-out can be classified into two parts: early interventions and later interventions. The early interventions included intermediary activities by Clarence Farmer, Father Paul Washington, the Tuesday Night Group, and Joel Todd. The later interventions were by Monsignor Charles Devlin and others, and the City-wide Community Coalition for Human Rights.

CLARENCE FARMER AND FATHER PAUL WASHINGTON

From 1975 on, Clarence Farmer, a black executive director of the Philadelphia Commission on Human Relations, kept in close contact with MOVE. Farmer said that practically every week MOVE members would come to his office to talk through their problems.

MOVE people, in addition to having their own ideas, concepts and feelings, always felt they were totally misunderstood by everybody . . . I wanted to make sure they could come to my office, sit down with me and talk about issues and concerns they had. . . . They knew they could always come to my office; and I would sit and talk to them; give them time and attention.

Sometimes Farmer was able to help. For instance, he helped them form a nonprofit corporation that received funding for a community project.

Farmer also assigned a black field staff worker, Gloria Sutton, to be available to communicate with MOVE. He used his influence to intercede on MOVE's behalf with other parts of city government. During the May 20, 1977, confrontation between MOVE and the police, Farmer, along with Father Paul Washington, helped bring about a disengagement.

Father Washington, the rector of the Church of the Advocate in North Philadelphia, was a highly visible and involved black clergyman. He had a long acquaintance with MOVE people. He recalled how he came to know them:

My wife, who often looked at televised meetings of the Board of Education, told me that for the last two or three meetings, individuals representing this group would often disrupt the meetings and charge [the board] with miseducating and misguiding the children whom they were charged with educating.

She added they all spoke well, intelligently, and were quite articulate. I found that they had a telephone. I called their residence. I told them that . . . I wanted to know something about them and what they represented. Eleven members of MOVE came, and for the next two and half hours, it was not a dialogue nor a situation where I could ask questions. It was all, "We were taught by John Africa this and that, etc. . . . "[1]

From that time on, MOVE frequently asked Father Washington to observe their trials and take them to the House of Corrections to visit their members who were in jail. He observed:

As a clergyman, I could go at all times and was permitted to take Robert Africa in with me. I wrote many letters in their defense because I observed that frequently their rights were violated because they were members of MOVE; although, in most instances, they had provoked the situation which led to their arrests or their being ejected from various gatherings.

I would say that I was perhaps one of the closest sympathizers, defenders and supporters of this group at this time in this unfolding saga of MOVE in Philadelphia.[2]

After a while, Father Washington's relationship with MOVE deteriorated. MOVE members began to use abusive language when he was unable to transport them to the House of Corrections whenever they needed to go there. "From that time on, I continued to be involved with situations pertaining to MOVE where I felt the city or the police were over-reacting and at times were violating the rights of MOVE; although I often felt that MOVE was provoking the situation."[3]

On May 20, 1977, he received a call from a Powelton neighbor saying that hundreds of people had gathered on the street near the MOVE residence, and the police were there. The incident had started when a MOVE member had been evicted from a nearby apartment and a scuffle had arisen with the police. Washington went to the MOVE house and talked to Delbert Africa. He found out that MOVE had heard that Chuck Africa had been arrested and brutally beaten. MOVE was enraged, and members were parading up and down the porch of their house, brandishing guns.

Washington described his intervention:

I went and told the Police Commissioner Delbert's story. He denied that Chuckie was beaten. I went back and told Delbert that the Commissioner had denied it. He insisted that if they could not see Chuckie and be assured that he was whole and in one piece there would be trouble. I relayed Delbert's statement to the Commissioner.

The Commissioner made a deal, he would send for Chuckie, expose him to everyone so that he could be seen, but in return he wanted MOVE to surrender the guns which they had in the house. I went and told Delbert that we had a deal, to which Delbert answered: "Like hell! We don't just want to see Chuckie, we want him released, then they will get the guns." Here the negotiations broke down.[4]

Father Washington, reflecting on this experience, realized that he could not help them negotiate. He saw negotiation with MOVE as being impossible because they would keep raising the stakes: "The instances which I have cited as well as others which I had heard led me to conclude that for them 'the system' was not an entity with which they could negotiate, tolerate or endure. I felt that they could never make peace with what they saw as oppression."

Delbert Africa confirmed Washington's analysis but added more to the picture. First, he commented that he never promised to give up the weapons, but to "start working on that." Delbert added that the issue of the guns enhanced MOVE's bargaining position, and they were going to take maximum advantage of it:

Obviously, the police's main concern was the weapons. Frankly, MOVE knew we had them over a barrel with that. We were going to lever as much as we could. The more we get them talking, we could start talking about Jerry, Conrad, and Bob coming home [from prison, where they were being held on charges arising from the 1976 clash with the police].

In effect, Delbert agreed with Washington's analysis that MOVE did not intend to stop the confrontation after seeing Chuck. MOVE escalated the demands to bring attention to its underlying issue: the release of the "political prisoners." With the advantage of hindsight, it can be seen that there were both surface and hidden issues in this transaction, and that the intervenor was working on the surface ones. MOVE was not willing to disengage until its primary concern of release of its leaders was addressed.

Delbert pointed out a second problem, the site where Chuck's inspection was to take place:

[Washington] told me Chuck was just down Pearl Street in the car. I told him I don't want him down there at the car. "You are crazy. Hell, I'm not going down there. Bring him here [to the MOVE house]." Inspector Fencl said that was not going to happen. His fear was that we were going to snatch Chuck up. My fear was that I would be snatched. I had no trust in the police whatsoever, based on their past history.

Clarence Farmer was also called in to help in this confrontation. When he arrived, MOVE and the police were exchanging insults. He found that Father Washington was already on the scene. He and Washington agreed that their task was to disengage the parties. They succeeded in calming the police and MOVE, and finally the 200 policemen withdrew. The open

confrontation was replaced by a siege with round-the-clock surveillance by about 100 plainclothes police.

THE TUESDAY NIGHT GROUP

As the crisis began to grow during 1977, neighborhood involvement became more intense. Some neighbors formed the
Tuesday Night Group, which met regularly to explore ways to
deal with the community's conflict with MOVE as well as the
conflict among the neighbors themselves. They tried to canvass
the positions of every neighborhood organization, including
MOVE, and developed a "fact sheet" that they distributed to
the residents of Powelton Village. The purpose was to give every
group the viewpoints of the other groups and to use the document as a basis for discussion.

They also developed a document titled "Principles of Being
a Good Neighbor," which tried to define the rights and obliga-
tions of neighbors. The document was to be discussed in the
hopes of reaching consensus among all groups. Among other
things the document proposed the following principles:

—All neighbors have the right to different beliefs, cultural diversity
  and to live together irrespective of religion, race or philosophy.
—All neighbors have the right and obligation to solve problems of
  neighbors at the community level.
—All members of our community have a right to a home [referring to
  the old, the blacks, the poor, communes, and other neighbors that
  were being driven out of the area by land speculators].
—All neighbors have a right and obligation to speak out [referring to
  the involvement of the police in community affairs].[5]

The Tuesday Night Group held weekly meetings to provide
a forum for all factions of the neighborhood to air their grievances and discuss their views. However, the discussions were
disrupted when MOVE supporters and some of the more ec-
centric neighbors began to monopolize the floor. The Tuesday
Night Group brought in outside facilitators to ensure better exchanges in the meetings. Through Quaker contacts, they invited George and Lillian Willoughby, who were involved in the

Movement for a New Society. This group was a New Left, peace-oriented, community-building organization. The Willoughbys and the Movement for a New Society were in the forefront in applying conflict-resolution skills to community problems. They established meeting procedures that helped the group stay together.

Various members of the Tuesday Night Group were also attempting to involve outside agents, such as hostage crisis experts from Washington, D.C., and representatives of the Philadelphia Commission on Human Relations. The Commission, which had a broad mandate to intervene in all group conflicts and act as community mediator or fact finder, sent Gloria Sutton to work with them. One member of the group described Sutton as " . . . a nice person who meant well, but she was not up to this. All she did was listen to us." Sutton, however, consistently maintained contact with MOVE and its neighbors from the mid-1970s through 1985.

Some members of the Tuesday Night Group were able to successfully negotiate two agreements with MOVE. One dealt with the garbage and rat problem. MOVE agreed to recycle its waste by composting it. This was an accepted organic gardening technique for turning vegetable matter into soil. It was a mutually satisfactory solution since it was in accord with MOVE's philosophy, and at the same time reduced the odor and rat population for the neighbors. MOVE also entered into a written accord in which they promised not to threaten members of the community.

Delbert Africa cited the composting agreement as an example that MOVE did indeed respond to neighborhood concerns. "We said, if it bothers you, we'll turn it over, and we turned over our whole yard down to about two feet; we got some exercise doing it." According to Jim Quinn of *Philadelphia Magazine*, "[By] the summer of 1977 the odor problem [in the neighborhood] had really diminished."[6] However, by that time the police involvement in the conflict had escalated to such a level that the neighbors hardly noticed whether MOVE had complied with the agreement. A lengthy PUN report devoted only two sentences to monitoring the agreement which read: "[They] have begun to turn their garbage. . . . The smell and health hazard have been significantly reduced."[7] Most of the neighbors, by that time, were so consumed with the issue of how to deal with the massive police presence and danger of violence that the issue of the cleanliness of MOVE's premises seemed minor in comparison. However, MOVE members pointed to this agreement as evidence that they could negotiate in good faith and live up to an agreement that protected their interests as well as those of the other party.

JOEL TODD

A young white attorney, Joel Todd, acted as an intermediary as the MOVE conflict with the city began to come to the forefront. His involvement started in February 1977, when he was a court-appointed lawyer for one of the three MOVE members involved in the April 1976 fight with the police. He had spent some time getting to know them and listening to their concerns. By October 1977 he saw that MOVE and the city had reached a standoff. Police surveillance was in full force, and MOVE was holed up inside its headquarters.

Todd said that he was approached by a messenger, a neighborhood MOVE supporter, who asked him to serve as a go-between. Whether this invitation actually came from MOVE is unknown. Delbert Africa, MOVE's negotiator at that time, was unaware of this request. He stated that he accepted Todd's offer to intervene because he felt Todd was a good man. His opinion was based on the relationship they had built during the trials.

Todd had access to many resources to help him. His law firm was headed by a senior Democratic congressman, Joshua Eilberg, who had many political contacts in Philadelphia. The district attorney, Edward Rendell, was one of Todd's personal friends.

Todd's goal was to defuse a potentially violent situation. He saw the main parties as MOVE and the city administration. He said, "The neighborhood didn't have anything to do with this." According to some observers, there were some factors at the time that might have persuaded both MOVE and the city to consider negotiation rather than to stay locked in the standoff.

Joel Todd Negotiates with Delbert Africa

Source: Bulletin/Temple University Photojournalism Collection

The Phoenix, a short-lived neighborhood newspaper, pointed out that the city was spending large sums to maintain a 24-hour guard. At the same time, MOVE was pressured by their inability to leave their house because of the police presence. The approaching cold season threatened the well-being of MOVE members, whose house was unheated. MOVE heated with wood and cooked over an open fire, but firewood was becoming scarce. MOVE was also running short of food. During the early months of the confrontation, supporters brought in food, but most of the sympathizers were themselves poor and could not keep feeding MOVE indefinitely. *The Phoenix* noted that Inspector George Fencl of the Civil Affairs Division of the Philadelphia Police Department initiated some negotiations, which he called plea-bargaining. But it seems that this attempt went nowhere.[8]

In January 1978, a few months after Todd became involved, the new district attorney, Ed Rendell, took office. Todd saw the assumption of this office by a new person as a ripe opportunity. He felt that as "a new boy on the block," Rendell might be able to start with a clean slate since everybody else was "frozen." Todd appealed to Rendell to become actively involved.

As Todd was conveying positions back and forth between MOVE and the city, he evolved a proposal that contained these provisions:

1. MOVE members would individually submit to arrest and processing on outstanding charges [most of the charges arose from the May 20, 1977, gun display incident].
2. The city would favorably consider releasing on their own recognizance [without bail] those who submitted to arrest on the outstanding warrants.
3. MOVE would remove all people and animals from its headquarters.
4. MOVE would turn over its arms and submit to a complete lawful search and health code inspection.
5. MOVE would vacate the premises and not reside within two miles of the area.

These proposals were not acceptable to MOVE. According to *The Phoenix*, MOVE's position around this time was as follows:

1. Philadelphia and federal law officers should recommend release of the MOVE members pending trial without the necessity of posting bond [this point referred to the outstanding charges against MOVE members in the house].

2. MOVE would surrender, but its attorney and other third-party observers, acceptable to both MOVE and the city, would be present at every stage of the processing and detention of each arrested person.*

3. Surrender of people would be staggered so that MOVE's children could be cared for by MOVE members according to their own lifestyle.

The article added that MOVE had offered to invite unarmed police inspection of their premises to make sure that no weapons remained after the surrender. A similar invitation "might also be extended to representatives of the Department of [Licenses and Inspection] who were concerned with health, safety, and building code matters."[9]

However, according to Todd, "That was not a full statement of what MOVE was after. Those were the things they were asking with respect to themselves . . . if they surrendered. But that was not what prompted the confrontation to begin with, and that is not what they were demanding behind the scenes." Behind the scenes, they demanded the release of their imprisoned members. That, Todd pointed out, was considered unacceptable. "The city always held 'under no circumstances are we going to release three convicted, sentenced people.' And MOVE was saying, 'You've got to.' So we never got off the dime on that point. They were talking past each other."

The other issue that was difficult to reconcile in the two proposals was the city's insistence that MOVE relocate outside the city: "If you come out and surrender, you are going to have to agree not to go back into the house." Todd continued, "The city was insistent on that. MOVE was saying, 'Well, we're not going to agree to that.'"

Negotiations did progress on the issue of the extent to which

---

*This provision was designed to guarantee that MOVE members would not be beaten or abused while in custody.

the city could commit itself to releasing MOVE members without bail if they would submit to arrest on the outstanding charges. Many of these charges arose from the May 20, 1978, incident in which MOVE put on an armed display. The charges were rioting, inciting to riot, failure to disperse, disorderly conduct, terroristic threats, and possession of instruments of crime. All were misdemeanors except for rioting, which was a felony. Todd felt from private conversations that the city was willing to consider release without bail for the surrendering MOVE members.

In the midst of the negotiations, however, news reached MOVE that two of its imprisoned members had been beaten by the police. Todd said, "I saw two men who were injured; one of them still had dried blood on him. Another had pain while he was walking. . . . MOVE members [had been] cautiously optimistic about settling their dispute with the city until they received word of the incident in the jail."[10] MOVE members started asking for federal, state, and local investigations into the beatings. Soon after, Delbert Africa was reported to have shouted through his loudspeaker, "We are through negotiating, we don't trust them, they are untrustworthy."[11]

The negotiations broke down at this point. The city then went to Judge DiBona and requested an order authorizing the blockade of MOVE's premises by cutting off water, food, and other supplies. The stated purpose was to arrest MOVE members as they came out of the building. Mayor Rizzo was reported to have stated that the blockade would "attempt to starve them out." The court granted the order. At this juncture, Todd said, he was contacted by moderate elements in the city, who urged him to file a petition to stay the order and give negotiations one more chance, which he did.*

With the stay as a final opportunity to break the impasse, Todd attempted to arrange a face-to-face negotiation conference in Judge DiBona's chambers. The city manager, City Solicitor Sheldon Albert, State Supreme Court Justice Robert Nix, Jr. (whose order stayed the proceedings), Todd, and a negoti-

---

*David Kairys, PUN attorney, commented that he initially filed the petition for a stay. Todd made an additional filing.

ating team from MOVE headquarters were to attend the conference. A problem developed when the MOVE team refused
to leave its premises to go to court for the negotiations. Although the court and the city assured safe passage to the MOVE
delegation, MOVE refused. Todd tried bringing Justice Nix to
the MOVE house to persuade them to come.

Monsignor Devlin of the Cardinal's Commission on Human
Relations offered to accompany the MOVE team to ensure safe
passage. All attempts failed. According to the *Philadelphia Daily
News*, Delbert Africa is reported to have declared: "MOVE didn't
trust police, but would attend the hearings [negotiation session]
only if they could carry their own weapons with them. 'Africas
weren't going to place themselves in jeopardy of some maniac
ass cop who has our name on his bullet!' "[12]

Mediators had different explanations about why the MOVE
members refused the safe-conduct. Some interpreted it as genuine fear of the police, while others saw it as part of MOVE's
confrontational strategy, and still others construed it as MOVE's
sense of futility about what might come out of the negotiation
process. According to Monsignor Devlin, who played an intermediary role later, "[MOVE members] were afraid that once
they were out, the police would nab them and they would never
return to their house, or it was not politically advantageous to
them to respond. It was not in the agenda of confrontation."

Delbert Africa recalled,

My perception was the people I was dealing with were slimy. I could
very well see going down [to the courtroom], having a closed meeting,
and next thing I come out of there in shackles and handcuffs. The
only way anyone [would] know anything about it is they could tell the
press, "[initially] we were going to send him back to the house, but he
punched somebody while he was there, so we had to lock him up for
that." In our guidelines John Africa teaches us, "A politician ain't
nothing but a liar."

After the safe-conduct offer failed, MOVE suggested another alternative: that Robert and Conrad Africa be brought
from their jail cells to the courtroom cell to negotiate for MOVE.
The city agreed, and Robert and Conrad Africa met with the

negotiators from the city. Once again, progress was not possible. The main point of disagreement was MOVE's lack of trust if their people surrendered, they would be released without bail. They wanted a written commitment.

Todd remarked that the city people said in private that if MOVE members surrendered, bail would in fact not be a big issue; only if they said it publicly would it create a precedent. Todd believed the city, but MOVE did not trust it. Neither side could grant that the other was honorable. At this point Todd's intervention seems to have been stymied.

After this attempted negotiation session failed, Todd filed an affidavit with the court stating how inflammatory newspaper articles made negotiation difficult. These reports accused the city of spending millions of dollars for the surveillance of MOVE and claimed that a SWAT team was preparing to raid them. He also pointed out that there were

. . . serious and substantial negotiations. No agreement in fact had been reached, but several important issues had seemed to be resolved and there was the possibility of a negotiated, peaceful settlement. After the events outlined above MOVE's position hardened and negotiations were stalled.

If the intensity of the immediate confrontation and the carnival atmosphere could be abated, a negotiated, non-violent settlement may well be attainable within a reasonable period of time.[13]

Todd recalled, "I was sensing that both sides were starting to make movement, but neither side ultimately made the final movement to close the gap. It got awful close."

OBSERVATIONS ON TODD'S APPROACH AND STRATEGY

Todd's approach to the newly elected district attorney illustrates an important strategy concerning the timing of third-party intervention. Often a change of leadership or other important personalities among the parties opens the way for changes in attitude. New people may not feel committed to the objectives of the previous leadership, and thus may be amenable to peaceful third-party intervention. Such occasions may therefore provide a valuable opportunity for conflict-resolution efforts.

Throughout the negotiations, Todd saw his role purely as a mailbag:

I went to MOVE and said, "What is your position?" I went to the city and said, "This is what MOVE says." The city would give me a response, I would take the response back. I didn't try to influence their thinking. I did not try to tell them what was reality. I did not try to get into the situation to give them the benefit of my thinking of how to resolve the situation to get what they wanted. I tried scrupulously to maintain a position of trying to communicate what one side was saying and what the response to that was. Through the entire process, I maintained entire respect of both sides for the ability to exactly say what they want and no more. [I] didn't solve the problem. . . . and the reason is that it is not always just a matter of communication.

Even though Todd may have perceived his role merely as a mailbag, it may not have been understood that way by people with whom he negotiated. Such a role is different from the behavior usually expected of lawyers. City Solicitor Sheldon Albert, with whom Todd negotiated, commented:

When lawyers deal with lawyers, they assume the other lawyer has authority from his client. They assume he knows what the bottom line is when he goes into a meeting. He tries to get [a favorable concession] but knows he cannot go below a [bottom line]. Why would a guy agree [to negotiate with such a person] if he doesn't have the authority? It wasn't until we saw that nothing ever occurred that Joel said, "Listen, I'm just a go-between."

Moreover, the role of mere message carrier limits the intervenor's ability to help the parties find solutions to problems, especially in a situation where there are major perceptual and communication barriers between them. When Todd began by asking each party, "What is your position?" he might have unintentionally reinforced their commitment to their positions instead of encouraging them to focus on articulating the problem that was the source of their conflict. James Laue argues that helping the parties to analyze their dispute and define the underlying issues is an important step toward moving them to a problem-solving orientation.[14]

Todd also found it difficult to overcome gaps in trust between MOVE and the city. MOVE would not trust a guarantee of safe passage sufficiently to become involved in face-to-face negotiations. MOVE could not believe city assurances that its members would be released after surrender and processing. A question arises about whether, in this situation, an intervenor who functions only as a message carrier, or a mail bag, is at a disadvantage. Might a third party have been more effective in bridging the trust gap if he or she saw the intermediary's role to include the formulation and suggestion of new solutions, as well as, the interpretation of each party's messages in a manner that is more understandable and less threatening to the other?

Another side of the trust problem was the question of neutral turf. This quandary arose earlier, in Father Washington's attempted mediation, when the police were reluctant to bring Chuck Africa to MOVE headquarters for fear of MOVE grabbing him back and Delbert Africa was afraid to go down the street to see Chuck for fear of being kidnapped himself.

Another forum problem occurred when Todd attempted a face-to-face negotiation in Judge DiBona's courtroom. The courtroom is the monument of the establishment and represents the criminal justice system about which MOVE was complaining. It is unrealistic to expect parties who are defined as antiestablishment or counterculture to feel comfortable in that situation. On the other hand, as Delbert Africa admitted, it would be politically difficult for city officials to be seen going to MOVE headquarters to negotiate. A question arises whether the result might have been different if a face-to-face meeting at a neutral site had been arranged. The site would have had to be one that would have given MOVE members confidence in their physical safety and would have protected city officials from the public spotlight.

Todd also encountered difficulty because of the diversification of authority on the side he called "the City." Housing and health code violations were under the jurisdiction of City Solicitor Sheldon Albert. District Attorney Edward Rendell held decision-making authority over whether criminal charges would be filed. He had the power to take the initiative in requesting release on recognizance instead of bail. The court held decision-making power on matters submitted to it. Hence, each could disclaim responsibility for major pieces of the puzzle. For example, City Solicitor Albert said, "It was made crystal clear that the city could not enter into any kind of agreement, written, tacit, oral, or anything else, that people accused of a crime could be released without bail. It was beyond our power."

In fact, as District Attorney Ed Rendell recounted, informal understandings between each of these participants were made. However, the interest of each subdivision on "the City" side had to be acknowledged and coordinated to produce the basis for a workable agreement. It is possible that Todd's references to "the City" as a unified entity may have made it more difficult for him to address the specific interest of each division.

Leaving aside the process questions, the actual terms of the agreement Todd was working on raised many questions. His proposed agreement would have met the city's fundamental demand—removing MOVE from the city. However, it would not have addressed MOVE's primary concern—the release of the prisoners. This imbalance may have arisen in part because of Todd's definition of his role when he entered the conflict. Since he saw his main goal as averting violence, his energy was focused on disengaging the crisis instead of formulating a settlement that would accommodate the concerns of the two parties. It is puzzling that an examination of those issues was not included in the negotiations, considering Todd's view that many of the charges against the three imprisoned MOVE members were flimsy.

Some warn about the possible danger in mediating between two parties of unequal power. According to James Laue, mediation could sometimes work against the interest of the weaker one because the more powerful party often tries to use mediation to co-opt, subvert, cool out, or get intelligence on the weaker group.[15] A mediator who is not constantly aware of this possibility may wind up serving the interests of the more powerful. Todd's proposals would have supported the city's position while MOVE's primary interests were not addressed.

With hindsight, Todd reflected that one lesson he learned

from the MOVE experience was that "Anyone about to be involved in this type of situation has got to be a real clear-thinking individual. He has got to be able to filter out all the extraneous garbage." Todd also added that it took him a long time to accept that MOVE members were prepared to die for their cause. He believed that the city was not aware of the extent of MOVE's commitment: "When I finally accepted it, I became more of an agitator behind the scene, saying, 'Guys! You got to get this resolved, because if you don't, it is going to end in disaster.' When I understood that MOVE was prepared to die, I begged the city to back off." Todd believed, during the period he intervened, that the city exercised tremendous restraint and bent over backward both to prevent bloodshed and to accommodate MOVE without compromising the city's law-and-order image.

NOTES

1. Paul M. Washington, "My Experience with MOVE, Philadelphia, 1975–1986," paper presented at Third National Conference on Peacemaking and Conflict Resolution, Denver, June 6, 1986.

2. Ibid.

3. Ibid.

4. Ibid.

5. Tuesday Night Group, "Draft Statement of Human Rights in the Community," April 3, 1978. (Mimeographed.)

6. Jim Quinn, "The Heart of Darkness," *Philadelphia Magazine* 69, no. 5 (May 1978): 275.

7. PUN, "Statement and Report of Powelton United Neighbors, July 19, 1977." (Mimeographed.)

8. *The Phoenix*, November 1977.

9. Ibid.

10. David Gunter, "MOVE Kills Surrender Deal," *The Evening Bulletin*, Feb. 27, 1978, p. E6.

11. Ibid.

12. Kitty Caparella, "MOVE Refuses to Go to Court," *Philadelphia Daily News*, Mar. 2, 1978, p. 3.

13. Joel Todd, affidavit, March 8, 1978.

14. James H. Laue, "Third Party Roles in Community Conflict: The MOVE Experience," *Conflict Resolution Notes* 4, no. 2 (Sept. 1986): 13.

15. Ibid.

6

Third-Party Intervention:
Later Period

After Todd's intermediary effort failed, the court ordered MOVE's eviction. The plan was to establish a full blockade and starve out the members, in order to arrest them. As news spread that the blockade was going to be imposed, MOVE sympathizers rushed to supply MOVE with food and provisions. "Boxes packed with food, water containers, clothing, bedding, and candles were handed over the high wooden barricade erected by the MOVE members.[1] On March 16, 1978, 1,000 police sealed off a four-block area.[2] Police covered a truck with sandbags, armed it with machine guns, and pulled it up before MOVE headquarters. They stationed sharpshooters in the surrounding buildings. This deployment heightened the crisis and precipitated a new flurry of intermediary efforts.

MONSIGNOR CHARLES DEVLIN

One intermediary effort was by Monsignor Charles Devlin of the Cardinal's Commission on Human Relations, an agency under the auspices of the Catholic diocese. Devlin, an Irish Catholic priest, had cooperated with the police for over 20 years in calming potentially dangerous community situations. Rufus Cornelsen, of the Metropolitan Christian Council, suggested that he and Devlin should see if they could do anything in the MOVE crisis because of the possible threat to life. Devlin pointed out that his reason for intervening was to avoid bloodshed and the loss of life.

Devlin and Cornelsen talked to Phil and Delbert Africa. They apparently entered the scene when Joel Todd was trying to persuade MOVE to accept "safe passage" to the negotiating session in court. Devlin offered to accompany the MOVE people as a witness and a guarantor of safe passage. However, MOVE declined the offer. Later, when Robert and Conrad Africa were brought out of prison and negotiation was attempted in Judge DiBona's courtroom, Devlin and Cornelsen attended the session. Devlin said that the judge urged MOVE to use Devlin's good offices.

Devlin primarily carried messages between MOVE and the Office of the City Manager, talking mostly with Delbert "in long sessions lasting well into the night." Devlin said that in the process he put together a proposed settlement similar to Todd's.

Devlin saw himself as a message carrier. He stated, "MOVE never accepted the term, 'negotiator'; they did their own negotiating." He felt he had no power to help either party reformulate the proposals, test them against reality, or invent new approaches. Among other things, he was trying to get MOVE to agree to remove the children from the building before any violence erupted. MOVE, however, would not agree.

Although Devlin dealt primarily with Delbert Africa, he knew that any proposal had to be presented to some other people within MOVE before it would be binding. He assumed John Africa held the key to ratifying agreements. He saw Delbert "as one you could talk sense to," but "toward the end Delbert may have lost control to more irrational leadership."

Devlin did not meet the neighborhood groups. He talked only with MOVE and the city. He explained that under the Rizzo administration the city officials, the office of the District Attorney, and the police were so closely allied that to deal with the City Manager's Office was really to reach all of them.

Devlin had close law enforcement contacts and was privy to "confidential information" he would not reveal. He hinted, however, that MOVE was in fact a revolutionary organization.

A crisis arose during the period of Devlin's intervention. He was informed confidentially that MOVE felt that one of their members in the blockaded house, Ishongo Africa, was an in-former, and that MOVE would kill him if a confrontation with the police developed. Devlin said that he secretly managed to arrange for Ishongo to escape while he was negotiating with Delbert at the MOVE headquarters.

After Ishongo's defection,* Devlin returned to the MOVE residence to talk with Delbert Africa. He said, "I told you when I first came down here two things. Number one, I am here only because I see this as a threat to life, and I am interested in the preservation of life; and number two, I will never lie to you. What do you want to know about Ishongo?"

He answered all Delbert's questions. Devlin later observed, "I think there was a lot of respect that they showed me. Up until the day of the actual shoot-out, they never used obscenities or foul language towards me."

Devlin withdrew in April 1978 when the Citywide Coalition for Human Rights took over the intermediary function, and Oscar Gaskins obtained a written power of attorney to repre-sent MOVE in the negotiations. Devlin said that he did not share the settlement proposals he had been working on with the Gas-kins team because he felt that acknowledging their existence to anybody would have been a violation of confidentiality.

Phil Africa had a different evaluation of Monsignor Devlin's intervention. He felt Devlin was a police agent. "He talked like the police. He can wear a collar, but his closeness with the po-lice was so much, we picked it up. [He had] the same attitudes as the police." Phil added that half the time MOVE refused to talk to Devlin.

OTHER INTERVENORS

Even while these mediation efforts were in progress, other kinds of interventions were also taking place. MOVE called on several individuals to intervene who were active in the civil rights movement and had clout. They also mentioned some black me-dia personalities as possible intervenors. One who tried was black

*Ishongo, later in an interview with the media, denied that he was defecting when he left the MOVE compound.[3]

activist and comedian Dick Gregory. He talked to MOVE once in Powelton. Gregory said, "[I] came to Philadelphia at the request of MOVE to possibly avert any bloodshed." MOVE asked Gregory to represent them in its negotiations with the city. Gregory's plan was to meet with MOVE, Judge DiBona, and District Attorney Rendell, and "give several press conferences between the meetings."[4]

Apparently Gregory's effort produced no results. The *Philadelphia Tribune* reported, "Dick Gregory disappointed neighbors and city officials when he announced that . . . he came to Philadelphia only to 'listen to both sides.' After conferring with MOVE and city officials, Gregory said he would return if either side requested his presence."[5] He never did.

The Philadelphia Yearly Meeting of the Society of Friends (Quakers) assigned a staff person, Charles Walker, to find how Quakers could be of service in this crisis situation. Walker and his colleagues established a round-the-clock vigil at the police barricade. They called it the Friendly Presence. By their witness they attempted to defuse tensions and inhibit provocative action. The Friendly Presence sought a peaceful solution to the problem and indicated that they were "working to solicit ideas for a possible basis of meaningful negotiations."[6] This presence lasted a month, until the final confrontation. Walker expressed frustration that they were unable to develop any new negotiating approaches.

A coalition of government-sponsored agencies also attempted to intervene. Bennie Swans of the Crisis Intervention Network (CIN) described how he initiated an intervention effort. His primary goal was to get MOVE out of the neighborhood without violence. The Network was a city agency with a primary mission of defusing Philadelphia's gang problem. According to Swans, the CIN field staff knew many MOVE members personally. Some had grown up in the same neighborhoods, others had met them through gang work. Moreover, MOVE in its early days had opposed gang violence and had cooperated with CIN by providing resource people for anti-gang workshops. Swans tried to involve Community Relations Service (CRS) and the Community Advocate's Office in his intervention attempt. CRS was a federal agency under the Department of Justice with broad experience in mediation and managing civil tensions. The Community Advocate's Office was a parallel Pennsylvania organization under the Attorney General's Office.

Frank Tyler, a CRS staff member, however, described their involvement as arising from a request by George Fencl, head of the Civil Affairs Division of the Philadelphia Police Department. Tyler organized a three-person negotiating team, two from the Community Advocate's Office and one from CRS, that talked with MOVE members in the house. They used a walkie-talkie since they could not get through the barricades.

The team then went to Judge DiBona to request permission to formally intervene, but the judge denied it. Tyler stated, "I never attempt to analyze a judge's decision. We never had an opportunity to talk and explain our position, so it was denied." That apparently ended the role of these agencies until after the August 1978 shoot-out. One wonders if the reason the judge denied them access might have been his desire to avoid a proliferation of third-party involvement, since he had already authorized Devlin's intermediary activities.*

Another attempted intervention was by an agency under the control of the state's governor. The *Sunday Bulletin* reported:

Governor Shapp's Civil Tensions Task Force had offered assistance to the City of Philadelphia to resolve the blockade in a peaceful manner. But the city, in the person of City Solicitor Sheldon Albert . . . rejected the offer. "There is no racial tension," Albert said in a telephone interview . . . "the situation is well in hand."[7]

THE CITYWIDE COMMUNITY COALITION FOR HUMAN RIGHTS

After Todd's attempt, one group that played a major intermediary role was the Citywide Community Coalition for Human Rights (CCCHR). Two people performed key parts in this intervention: Walter Palmer and Oscar Gaskins. Palmer was an established black businessman and a civil rights activist. He said

*Since Judge DiBona is now dead, the authors were unable to confirm this hypothesis.

that he had been approached by MOVE supporters to act as an intermediary between the city and MOVE because he knew some of the MOVE leadership, particularly Robert Africa. He also believed that he was a person MOVE could trust, since they perceived him as having connections. He was known for 20 years of aggressive campaigning against police abuse and for his activities in community development and self-help projects.

Palmer agreed to act as an intermediary. His primary stated goal was to disengage the confrontation over the blockade and achieve a settlement that met both parties' needs. Since there was a major power imbalance between the city and MOVE, he decided to form a force powerful enough to put pressure on the city to engage in serious discussions. He organized a coalition of black religious, political, business, and community leaders: the Citywide Community Coalition for Human Rights. The Coalition's role was to create a climate that would facilitate a negotiated settlement of the MOVE problem. It would also serve as an overseer and guarantor of any agreement that might be reached.

The leadership of the Coalition included State Representative David Richardson, attorney Oscar Gaskins, Sister Falakah Fattah, Reverend Leon Sullivan, and Father Paul Washington, with Palmer as the chairman.* Two committees were created: the Legal Committee and the Communications Committee. The former, headed by Oscar Gaskins, was charged with investigating the status of all criminal charges against MOVE and assessing any violations of MOVE's civil rights.

The Communications Committee, led by Palmer and Sister Fattah, was charged with working with the media, businesses, and civic leaders. Its strategy was to approach the media and provide it with stories that were favorable to what the Coalition was trying to accomplish. According to Palmer, "We tried to manage the news rather than be managed by it." They issued press releases and distributed a newsletter called "The Third

*Palmer may not have emerged in his central position from the very beginning, for one flier distributed in the neighborhood to invite people to attend the initial organizational meeting of CCCHR listed Father Washington, Councilman Blackwell, Sister Fattah, and State Representative David Richardson as conveners of the meeting.

Option." The purpose was to "get a hearing for MOVE on the blockade issues." According to Sister Fattah, "We felt that MOVE could not articulate their needs in such a way that other people can understand it. If this is not done, there can't be any resolution."

The Coalition took the position that the city's method of handling the conflict reflected a "continuing history of the flagrant disregard for the human rights of blacks at home and abroad."[8] Following this view, the coalition invited Andrew Young, U.S. ambassador to the United Nations, to come to Philadelphia as an observer and to discuss the human rights of the MOVE family.[9] Palmer went to the United Nations in New York, and through contacts with Third World delegates attempted to publicize the MOVE case as a human rights violation that needed to be investigated by the United Nations. This focused international media attention on Philadelphia, to the chagrin of city officials.

The Coalition also organized demonstrations denouncing the city's strategy for dealing with the MOVE problem. Once, according to Palmer, 15,000 people* formed a ring around City Hall, creating a human blockade to register their opposition to the police blockade of MOVE. Additionally, the coalition organized deliveries of food and other supplies through police lines for MOVE's children. Meanwhile, other coalition subcommittees met with civic leaders to press for settlement.

On another front, Palmer selected Oscar Gaskins of the Legal Committee to carry out the actual negotiations between MOVE and the city. Palmer teamed up with Gaskins when talking to MOVE was necessary. As a condition for assuming the role of MOVE's negotiator, Gaskins insisted on having MOVE sign a power of attorney so that it would be clear that he alone represented MOVE. Not only did the document distinguish Gaskins from earlier intervenors, it helped clarify his status as MOVE's negotiator. Until then, MOVE had always represented itself. The power of attorney gave evidence that MOVE had finally delegated authority to someone to represent its interests.

Gaskins saw his role as that of an attorney negotiating for

---

*According to some newspaper accounts, the number was much lower.

**Left to Right, Walter Palmer, Oscar Gaskins, Inspector
George Fencl**

Demonstrators King Philadelphia City Hall

Source: Bulletin/Temple University Photojournalism Collection

MOVE. He shuttled among MOVE's barricaded compound, the city's managing director, the Office of the Police Commissioner, and the mayor. He continued to work on the issues that had been formulated by Todd. Significantly, he was the first to seriously negotiate MOVE's primary demand, release of its prisoners. Even though it was the most important issue for MOVE, the city had deemed the demand nonnegotiable because it could not respond without compromising the integrity of the legal system and establishing a dangerous precedent.

Gaskins proposed a solution that could accommodate the interests of both parties. He suggested that the prisoners be allowed to appeal their sentences. The Superior Court could then release them on their own recognizance, which would allow them to be free until the appeal. Gaskins observed that the prisoners had already served most of their sentences anyway. If they won their appeal, they would not have to go back. If they lost, their sentences could be commuted to time served, or at the most they would go back for the short remainder of their terms. Gaskins arrived at this analysis through the work of the Coalition's Legal Committee, which had carefully documented the legal standing of all the cases. He offered this proposal as a way of breaking the deadlock. It was a breakthrough that saved face for both parties and was accepted by the city and MOVE.

After solving this problem, Gaskins was able to negotiate a settlement on other issues. The city took the additional step of agreeing to commit itself in writing to having MOVE members released on their own recognizance after submitting to arrest on the charges that arose from the May 20, 1977, confrontation. MOVE, in turn, agreed to vacate its premises. With these concessions made, the stumbling blocks to reaching a settlement were finally removed. An agreement was signed and filed in court on May 5, 1978, that contained the following terms:

1. Those members of MOVE for whom there are outstanding warrants will subject themselves to criminal judicial process by . . . accompanying police . . . for processing, arraignment and release on recognizance.

2. The city will remove the barricade sufficiently to allow food and water in to accommodate all the members of MOVE . . . [includ-

ing the animals]. During the processing procedures, said food and water will consist of one meal per person three times a day.

3. After the completion of the processing, MOVE will turn over to the city whatever arms, gunpowder, explosives that are presently on the premises.

4. After that is done, the city will begin to dismantle the barricades, allow access to MOVE members of food and visitors, and turn on the water and make a city trash truck available.

5. After 5 days, the city will inspect the premises for violations of city codes.

6. Within two weeks, MOVE will dismantle the platform in front of its house.

7. MOVE will remove all or subsequently all the animals living in the premises.

8. MOVE will not put garbage in its backyard.

9. MOVE will vacate the premises within ninety days. During that period, there will be a police presence maintained in the neighborhood and civil rights of both neighbors and MOVE will be protected.

10. MOVE agrees to permit Oscar Gaskins to represent them in court, and waives its personal presence in courtroom proceedings to avoid further confrontations.

11. The Citywide Black Coalition on Human Rights [CCCHR] and the Powelton United Neighbors support the agreement and agree to assist the city in effecting compliance with the agreement.

The agreement was signed by Judge DiBona, City Solicitor Sheldon Albert, and attorney Oscar Gaskins.

The agreement made no reference to releasing Jerry, Conrad, and Robert Africa. That had been accomplished by an oral arrangement and had already been carried out as a precondition to MOVE's assent to the May 5 agreement.

THE AGREEMENT: COMPLIANCE AND BREAKDOWN

MOVE and the city began to implement the agreement immediately after it was signed. All the MOVE members who had outstanding charges surrendered and were processed under Gaskin's supervision. They cleaned their building and allowed it to be searched and inspected. They allowed in health inspectors, who found the premises to be clean. In a thorough search for weapons only inoperative ones were found.[10] The city started dismantling the blockade and allowed food and other necessary items to come into the building.

However, points of contention developed over interpreting the agreement. The city insisted that MOVE must tear down the fence surrounding the compound, get rid of all the animals except a few puppies, and turn in its loudspeakers to the police. MOVE refused, stating that the agreement did not obligate them to do these things. Phil Africa told the judge, "We want to emphasize to you as strongly as possible that our interpretation of the agreement and that communicated to us by our lawyer was different from yours."[11] Gaskins agreed that the judge's demand was not part of the agreement. He threatened that he "would fight any such order and would file a petition to get Judge DiBona removed from the case if he followed through on the matter."[12] The controversy brought MOVE and Gaskins back to Judge DiBona's court, where the judge reiterated, "[It] was his understanding that the city and MOVE had agreed that it would be done within three weeks after the agreement was signed."

During the court session two MOVE members called the judge "a liar and bloodletter," which led to contempt citations. Gaskins had to mediate between the judge and the MOVE members. His solution was to draft a letter for the MOVE delegation that the judge interpreted to be an apology. Judge DiBona lifted the contempt citation.

Other controversies arose. MOVE claimed that unwritten promises exchanged during the negotiations of the May 5 agreement were being violated. One involved the controversy over how to handle the outstanding cases against the various MOVE members who had been charged in the May 20 armed confrontation and other incidents. Were they to be permanently freed outright, or were they required to stand trial? According to Jerry Africa, MOVE members signed the agreement because they believed that the city would drop all the "trumped-up" charges against them. He referred to oral assurances that city officials had given them. He argued that since it would look improper for the city to make this sort of agreement in writing, they committed themselves in a verbal understanding. He said that if MOVE had known that their release was going to be only temporary, they would not have signed the agreement.

Gaskins's view was that there were no oral agreements. However, he said:

Based on my experience and based on the conversation with the relevant negotiators from the District Attorney's Office, I thought that even if [the city and the D.A.] did not drop the charges, I never thought that they would result in any significant terms of prison. I thought they would get what people normally get: two years' probation, a year probation, that kind of thing.

Looking back, former District Attorney Ed Rendell agreed with Gaskins.

[The charges] were by and large misdemeanors. None of the MOVE members had prior records of violence. If the court had handled those cases as non cause célèbre cases, which they probably would have had the MOVE members not done the things that happened subsequently [breached the agreement and resisted eviction], they would have had every right to expect probation or a very short county prison sentence for some [of the charges].

These contradictory interpretations may reflect the different perspectives of attorneys and people who are not members of the legal profession. Experienced criminal lawyers like Gaskins and Rendell are accustomed to negotiating compromise or plea bargains for defendants. The bottom line for them is whether the person serves time. Defendants, particularly if they consider themselves innocent, are not only interested in freedom, but also in confirmation of their innocence.

Given these perspectives, Gaskins and MOVE could easily have interpreted the discussions about the May 20 charges to be consistent with their own perceptions. Gaskins could have told his clients that they prevailed. By that he meant he could keep them out of jail. The clients may have interpreted "they won" to mean they had been absolved of the crime.

A related problem was paragraph 10 of the agreement, in which MOVE members had waived their right to appear in court. Gaskins pointed out the reason for that:

The district attorney had always taken the position that these people had no prior criminal records and these charges, inciting to riot and the rest of that, did not appear to be that significant. Therefore, to avoid any confrontation, the district attorney agreed that they need not appear in court for any purpose. They did not have to come in for arraignment. They did not have to come in for continuances. They did not even have to attend their trials.

But, according to Gaskins, after the agreement was signed and MOVE started complying, the District Attorney's Office changed its mind and said, "I don't think we can do that, get your clients in the office." Then they began to press the charges and insist that MOVE people appear in court. Gaskins added:

They began to act as if those were very serious charges and started talking to the people in terms of lots of time in prison.

Once MOVE started complying with the agreement, it was reasonable to assume that the city's action represented a breach of the agreement. The city started moving on these charges just as if the MOVE members had committed murder. The whole thing began to break down . . . after that.

Another series of controversies involved the agreement to vacate the MOVE building within 90 days. The Coalition had tried to help MOVE find alternative locations to use after it vacated its Powelton residence. David Fattah, of the House of Umoja, a Muslim community center, indicated that a black farmer in New Jersey had made a rural site available. Fattah drove some MOVE leaders to the farm, and at that time they seemed excited by the opportunity of moving there. However, Fattah said that during the 90-day truce period, some MOVE members apparently had visited the farm on their own. On that visit they received the impression that the farmer wanted to use them for "slave labor." Thus, they rejected the offer. No one followed up to clarify what had happened on this second trip.

As the 90-day deadline approached, controversy arose over the meaning of the eviction clause of the agreement. The city took the position that all MOVE members must leave the premises by the ninetieth day. If they did not, they would be in violation of the agreement and subject to arrest.

MOVE claimed that the city had agreed to help them find another location and had not fulfilled its part of the agreement. Both Sister Fattah and Gaskins referred to this promise, pointing out that the city did not produce alternative locations. The Philadelphia Commission on Human Relations and other groups searched for alternative living premises. Clarence Farmer, the Commission's director, pointed out that his office was not able to raise sufficient money to purchase farm land for MOVE, but MOVE never knew that. Moreover, Lary Groth, Farmer's deputy, indicated that MOVE found fault with every option suggested.

Phil Africa described one plot of land that was offered as being surrounded on three sides by marsh. He rejected it because "I'm not taking my family into a place where I can't get out."

MOVE members also pointed out that MOVE independently had bought a house in Richmond and tried to purchase a farm in Charlotte County, Virginia. They had entered an agreement to buy a 96-acre farm for $12,000.[13] However, Sharon Cox described the pressure that was applied to run them off their property in Richmond.

Two days after we arrived in Virginia, a bunch of people came out to the house and said they had reports of children with no clothes . . . digging food out of the ground. They wanted to see the children, look at their birth certificates, have a doctor examine them. We said, "No." They came back with a court order. We got the house ready for confrontation. We nailed the door and windows shut and put a bullhorn in the front window. They were back surrounding the house. Cops on horseback . . . tear gas and rifles. One night they stormed the house and took the children off in a station wagon. We went to jail for three weeks and the children were sent to foster homes until the MOVE organization bailed us out.[14]

MOVE members suspected that the police in Richmond had been tipped off by the Philadelphia police, and that is why they were harassed. Thus, they felt they would not be free from harassment by the city even if they relocated.

Ramona Africa argued that under the right circumstances, MOVE would have wanted a rural location. She talked about the farm in Charlotte County:

We wanted to send our children on a farm because it is healthier, and it was land MOVE picked out. It wasn't isolated like the land the government would have picked out. The politicians deliberately sabotaged it, made us lose it, by going to Virginia and telling the people around the farm that MOVE would kill their cows, that we took drugs. . . . [Neighbors] complained to the realtor who, to keep us from getting the farm, demanded the full price for the farm in one payment, knowing we couldn't pay it, so we lost the farm.[15]

In short, both MOVE and city officials accused each other of impeding implementation of the relocation provision of the agreement.

MOVE's spokespeople, Jerry and Delbert Africa, further claimed that there were other verbal promises given by the city that were violated. They asserted that the 90 days for the evacuation was not an absolute deadline. There was a recognition that it might not be possible to relocate during that time, and that since MOVE was showing a good faith effort, the city should allow a longer period. As the 90-day deadline approached, Delbert Africa reportedly wrote to the City Council and Judge DiBona, asking for a time extension and for a relocation site that had been promised. The request was not granted.

The April 4, 1978, *Philadelphia Daily News* reflected the confusion and irony of this search for new quarters:

At least one of the five North Philadelphia houses offered to MOVE for taking rental for $1 [per] year has been declared unfit for human habitation. [The others were] run down properties. . . . The ludicrous thing is that the city is trying to drive the MOVE people out of this property on the claim that it is unfit for human habitation. But the same administration would be very happy to see them move into a situation up here [in North Philadelphia] which is far worse.

Gaskins pointed out that City Solicitor Albert was quoted in the press during this period as saying that the city would tear down the MOVE house as soon as it was vacated. Albert recalled that his reason was to "obliterate any rancor that would still be in the neighborhood, any reminiscing of what had occurred"—or, as the *New Republic* put it, "to prevent it from becoming a cult-type symbol."[16] Gaskins felt that Albert's statement incensed MOVE, since they did not consider tearing down the building to be part of the agreement. Gaskins filed a petition for an injunction to stop the city, but the building was razed before he could get a hearing.

Jerry Africa mentioned that during the negotiations, members were discussing renovating the building and turning it into a temple, an information center, or even a rental property. MOVE members interpreted the May 5 agreement as prohibiting the use of the headquarters for residential purposes, but they did not think they were restricted from using it for other purposes. Sheldon Albert, on the other hand, voiced the more common interpretation: "The agreement said 'vacate.' That is one of the few words in the English language that is not subject to more than one definition. They knew what 'vacate' meant, and they knew we would tear [the building] down."

On the ninety-first day, the city filed a petition with Judge DiBona requesting an eviction order. The judge ordered MOVE to appear and show cause why it should not be held in contempt. He instructed Inspector George Fencl to read the order over a loudspeaker at MOVE headquarters and tell the members to appear in court that afternoon.

MOVE members refused, on the ground that the May 5 agreement barred them from appearing in person. The court's position, according to Gaskins, was that violation of any term of the agreement voided the whole document. Therefore, the provision prohibiting the court from requiring MOVE's presence was no longer operative. The judge then granted the police a warrant to arrest all the people in the MOVE building. Six days after the order, 300 armed police officers and fire fighters arrived at the MOVE house to enforce Judge DiBona's order. It was apparent that violence was going to erupt.

At this point, Palmer again tried to intervene to avert the

looming crisis. He went to the basement of the house, to which MOVE members had retreated for protection, and talked with the leaders to see if violence could be avoided. He said he did not plead with them to come out, but described the magnitude of the forces arrayed outside and the probable consequences if MOVE decided to resist. They told him to go away. As he was leaving, something that sounded like a firecracker or gunshot exploded and the shoot-out began.*

Inspector George Fencl had telephoned Monsignor Devlin the night before, to ask him to try intervention one last time. In the morning Devlin went to the MOVE building and with the bullhorn tried to make them realize how great a danger they faced if they did not come out. He believed that MOVE thought he had "come down on the side of the police, but it was a question of getting them out." He then entered the building to talk to them. They were in the basement. A battering ram had smashed through a window of the house and had knocked down a porch, allowing the police to occupy the upper floors. Devlin said there was a "great amount of hysteria involved, especially with the women. The men were hollering, 'Just leave us alone.' "

He left 15 seconds before the firing started. There had been controversy about who started shooting first. In the ensuing exchange, however, one policeman died from a bullet that entered through his neck. Other police, fire fighters, and MOVE members were also wounded. At last MOVE surrendered, and as this was being televised, three policemen were filmed beating Delbert Africa and dragging him by his hair.

Within two hours after the surrender, city bulldozers razed the house. City Solicitor Albert justified the speedy demolition thus:

After the conflict that thing was dangerous. It was filled with water [and] half torn down anyway as a result of police battering. We were scared to death some kids would drown or get hurt playing there. . . . [On] Spring Garden Street, slightly to the north, a large group was

---

*Palmer testified in the subsequent MOVE trials that the shot did not come from the MOVE house.

gathering. They were going to march. And for those purposes I personally ordered it torn down.

STRATEGIES AND FACTORS THAT LED TO THE MAY 5 AGREEMENT

Even though the May 5, 1978, agreement did not prevent bloodshed, it was an important step that could have led to a peaceful settlement of the conflict. It was in itself a significant achievement. Therefore, it may be useful to examine the factors and intervention strategies that led to it.

One crucial factor was the willingness of the intermediaries to dedicate an extraordinary amount of time and energy to the mediation process. According to Palmer, "We literally almost lived in MOVE's compound six to nine months, day and night." Coalition members, as well as Todd, worked without pay. Others, such as Monsignor Devlin, had institutional support but had to neglect their ordinary duties.

Second, the leaders of the CCCHR, particularly Palmer, were acceptable to MOVE. Palmer knew some of their leaders personally, and the similarity of his cultural background to MOVE's enabled him to communicate in a style they understood. For instance, before getting involved as an intermediary, he told MOVE, "Don't play games with me. Either you are serious about doing something or you are not. The moment I find you are not serious, I back off. It is on you."

Palmer added, "Many times I had to scream and holler at them because they said yes to one thing, and would later say that is not what they said." He talked about a confrontation with a MOVE member "who shoved some profanities at me . . . and I went right after him." Palmer believed that his tough talk and the no-nonsense attitude were important in getting his points across.

Palmer gained MOVE's trust. "One of the things that is clear is that what I was telling them was the truth. They could count on it." This made other mediation tactics possible. "If I said, 'Hey, you are going over the razor's edge at this point,' they would understand." This provided MOVE members an opportunity to test the reality of their positions. At the same time,

Palmer and Gaskins were interpreting each party's messages in a way the other could understand.

Another strategy CCCHR used was empowerment. The Communications Committee tried to build public support for MOVE's position by using the media to explain MOVE's concerns. The committee organized public demonstrations against City Hall, and publicized the conflict in international forums. The Coalition's activities exerted political pressure on the city in a conflict where the city had previously had the upper hand. Even though neither Palmer nor Gaskins alone had leverage with the city, the very fact that they were acting under the umbrella of an organization of various political, religious, and racial groups no doubt made the city more inclined to be flexible and seek a negotiated solution to the problem.

Todd observed:

When the community which had some ability to have their voices heard stood up in unity and said "We want resolution to this" and showed some evidence through their actions and their use of Gaskins, I think that softened the city's position about its willingness to agree to certain terms and conditions that it had not previously been willing to agree to.

He added that the Coalition's involvement behind Gaskins made the city "go back with the calculators and pencil and come back with a little more favorable offer."

Todd also suggested that pressure may have worked both ways. He recalled that the city was more willing to go the extra mile for Palmer and Gaskins because city officials saw them as having the capability to influence MOVE. The city had had little reason to believe that Todd could assure that MOVE would comply with any agreement he negotiated. Palmer, on the other hand, was seen as having that authority because of his aggressive style and his backing by an active community organization with a stake in the settlement.

It was important, too, that Gaskins had insisted on getting a power of attorney from MOVE. In a period when many had been carrying messages for MOVE, Gaskins saw this document as giving him exclusive authority to negotiate for MOVE. This may have enhanced his effectivenes, since other intermediaries, such as Monsignor Devlin, dropped out of the proceedings at this point in response to the power of attorney.*

The power of attorney also put a buffer between the court and the city negotiators, and MOVE. MOVE was confrontational with the courts, which often resulted in melees with the sheriffs. Their tactics might also have inflamed the conflict even more and made dialogue more difficult if MOVE participated directly in the negotiation.

These observations suggest that in situations where there is a large degree of mutual intolerance between the parties, an indirect negotiation strategy might be more fruitful. However, indirect negotiation and mediation can raise another set of problems that will be examined later.

Another factor contributing to reaching an agreement was Gaskin's creative proposal that gave the parties a way out of the deadlock. MOVE's crucial demand was the release of its members who had been formally sentenced by the courts. This position created a situation in which compromise appeared impossible because the city felt it could not uphold the "dignity of the law" while releasing sentenced people. The city was apparently worried about setting a precedent. Gaskins developed a simple but very timely solution, apparently one not thought of by other intervenors. He proposed that the prisoners be allowed to appeal their sentences. They would then apply to the Superior Court for release on their own recognizance. Release while awaiting appeal is a common practice. This solution saved face for the city because it involved ordinary legal procedures and put the ultimate release decision on an independent higher court. At the same time, it also satisfied MOVE's need to free its leaders. Perhaps one reason Gaskins could interject this solution was that he assumed a role wider in scope than that of a mere neutral message bearer. He was the attorney-advocate for one party; playing the role of negotiator and mediator at the same time. This combination of roles may have helped him to realize that a settlement which did not address his client's fundamental concern would not be workable.

*The power of attorney may have cleared authority with the outside world, but apparently MOVE was continuing to urge Devlin to intercede for them.

FACTORS LEADING TO THE FAILURE OF THE
MAY 5 AGREEMENT

It is possible that the May 5, 1978, agreement failed because either or both parties deliberately scuttled it. There were other problems however, that independently could have caused the breakdown. One may have been that nobody was directly in charge of continued oversight during the implementation period. CCCHR and PUN were listed in the May 5 agreement as "agreeing to assist the city in effecting compliance." However, both organizations faded out soon after the settlement. The lack of implementation oversight manifested itself when it became clear that MOVE was unable to find a place to relocate, the city's assistance was not forthcoming, and the New Jersey farm offer was turned down. Perhaps communications could have been clarified if someone had followed up on the conversation between MOVE and the New Jersey farmer, in which MOVE people got the impression they would be used for "slave labor." Jerry Africa's view was that MOVE was pushed into an agreement. Once it was signed, and MOVE members submitted to the arrest process, no one paid any attention to their problems and concerns.

Intervenors cited two main reasons for the lack of oversight during this period. First, mediators were exhausted after nearly nine months of crisis negotiations. They had their own lives to tend. Todd, Devlin, Palmer, and Gaskins pointed out the inordinate amount of time and effort that was required, and how they had to sacrifice their jobs and other responsibilities. They were burned out. Sister Fattah of the CCCHR's Communications Committee added that when MOVE rejected the farm offer and "wanted to go back to the drawing board, the Coalition people were tired. They did not have any energy left to go through it again."

She also pointed out that although MOVE was initially grateful for the contribution and assistance they received from the Coalition, that gratitude soon turned to rejection. MOVE adopted the line that they were saved from disaster through the wisdom of John Africa. Many who had given their time and energy to achieve the settlement felt rebuffed and were less inclined to continue to be involved.

Another explanation for the failure of the agreement revolves around the perceptions of the parties and intermediaries about MOVE's negotiating strategy. First, according to Palmer, MOVE was very difficult to deal with because they told the intermediaries "a lot of half truths—only things that they wanted you to know." On top of that, Palmer said, MOVE was unreliable. "They may say yes now and later on change their mind and say no. They did not have a sense of commitment. They wanted to use anything to their own ends." Todd said, "They were committed to undo the system and therefore would respect the agreements that served them and reject the others. They did not have a sense of morality." Some have described MOVE's negotiation style as confrontational, unaccommodating, and irrational. Lary Groth of the Commission on Human Relations described MOVE as "rationally irrational." Under these circumstances, mediation can become difficult, especially if the process is indirect, because the intermediaries can lose their credibility with the second party if the first party's position keeps changing or becomes unreasonably inflexible.

Gaskins, who was the principal negotiator, said he did not have this problem when dealing with the MOVE leadership. He said that the people he dealt with were articulate and intelligent, and that they adhered to the agreement except for the eviction. The reason they did not relocate was because they had no place to go.

The "composting agreement" worked out between PUN and MOVE in 1977 may be another example of MOVE's living up to an agreement that met its needs as well as those of its neighbors. However, the inability of Powelton residents, and the rest of the city, to remember whether MOVE complied did nothing to change MOVE's reputation as incapable of keeping its word.

The indirect style of negotiation, which prevented face-to-face meetings, may have contributed to the implementation problems. Even though shuttle diplomacy may be a good mechanism to prevent tension and animosity from hindering negotiations, it is questionable how long indirect negotiation can continue if the intermediary's aim is to try to resolve the basic issues of the conflict. If the entire negotiation is by proxy, the parties may not fully understand the difficulties the negotiator encountered extracting concessions from the other party. Their unrealistic expectations of what could be gained may encourage them to stick to their positions and leave the burden of framing an acceptable agreement to the mediator. If the mediator plays a more active role in formulating the agreement, the parties may feel less restraint to breach the settlement by claiming to have been misled by the intermediary.

One example may be the controversy over the evacuation of the building after the 90-day deadline. Even though the agreement clearly specified evacuation within 90 days, MOVE people claimed that they were given assurances that it was not an absolute deadline. One wonders whether the indirectness of the negotiation may have contributed to MOVE's attitude that they were not bound by the agreement. Jerry Africa constantly referred to the settlement as "the city's agreement" or "Gaskins' agreement," instead of "our agreement."

Delbert Africa suggested that face-to-face meetings might have been more useful.

It is hard for any mediator to understand and get into the position of both people. I know it would be doubly hard, especially in MOVE, when our whole belief system is opposed to the belief system of most mediators. [For instance] it is hard for them to convey the importance we see in recycling vegetables back to earth. None of the intermediaries had the forcefulness that any MOVE member would have in addressing the issues.

On the other hand, he conceded, "If we got a mediator more in line with MOVE's belief systems, like some Rastafarians, he would not listen to what the city was saying."

The challenge for the intermediary, then, is to determine the points in the negotiation process where face-to-face negotiation might be counterproductive and where the parties have calmed down enough to start facing each other rationally. Direct negotiations often help the parties break down stereotypes and see each other as human beings with similar needs and constraints. This understanding, which was lacking in the MOVE conflict, can become the beginning for building trust. Trust is an important foundation for assuring implementation of the agreement.

Delbert Africa's comments underscore another point—the need for intervenors to be aware of the different ways that groups express conflict behavior. Mediators must find ways for the adversaries to see the issues that lie behind the communication styles. MOVE's public style of expressing conflict was highly charged. While many observers agree that MOVE generally did not initiate violence, its rhetoric was laden with aggressive threats. In confrontations with individual neighbors, MOVE members frequently threatened death or castration. Their diatribes over loudspeakers and in letters to city leaders were filled with talk of assassination. They alluded to supporters in other cities and countries who would rise up in retaliatory terrorism if MOVE was harmed.

These threats were an important part of the conflict. An elderly Powelton resident died of a heart attack, many neighbors felt, because of MOVE's aggressive rhetoric. As will be observed in the 1985 conflict, MOVE similarly threatened to assassinate the mayor, the police commissioner, and other officials. Then they claimed they had built underground tunnels and wired the entire neighborhood with explosives. At various times they threatened to blow up hotels and factories in Europe and other parts of the United States if their demands were not met. One never knew whether the threats were genuine. Jerry Africa, however, said threats were just a strategy: "One needed to look at MOVE's actions; MOVE never initiated violence."

Thomas Kochman, a communications analyst, suggests that there is a cultural difference in the significance of threats and the response to them in conflict situations. The line between "talking" and "fighting" is different between street-black and middle-class black and white cultures. To the middle class, angry words, heat, confrontation, insults, and threats will inexorably lead to violence. In street-black culture, however, he suggests there is a clearer separation. "Talking" is verbal. "Fighting" is physical. A "fight" begins when someone in an angry quarrel.begins to make a provocative [physical] movement.[17] Most observers pointed out that MOVE never physically provoked a confrontation.

Might the parties' and intervenors' conclusions about MOVE's dangerousness have been affected by their failure to understand the different way conflict is expressed in some subcultures? Laura Blackburne, president of the Institute of Mediation and Conflict Resolution in New York City, observed, "If you listened to the language and you did not hear the issues, then there would never be any discussion."[18]

Another problem is illustrated by the controversy over the handling of the MOVE house after the 90-day implementation period had expired. The city took the position that the house would be torn down. MOVE people claimed that, through Gaskins, a verbal agreement had been reached in which the city would not object to turning the house into a temple. Gaskins disagreed with MOVE's interpretation. However, he had no doubt that the May 5 agreement did not empower the city to tear down the house. There was no specific provision in the agreement covering this issue.

A major problem in writing agreements is clarity of terms. Here, the document did not provide a clear guideline. Oral understandings can be even more difficult. Christopher Mitchell argues that verbal addenda to mediated agreements are particularly dangerous and are to be avoided.[19] Were there oral addenda to the May 5 agreement? There are some indications to suggest that there were. Gaskins' initial major agreement with the city for the release of Jerry, Conrad, and Robert Africa pending appeal was an oral agreement. If MOVE's most important issue was resolved without any written agreement, one wonders if other issues might have been settled in a similar manner.

It also may be that MOVE interpreted some of the preliminary discussions it held as verbal commitments underlying the agreement. For instance, Delbert Africa referred to a face-to-face meeting he had with District Attorney Edward Rendell at which he claimed, "Rendell said . . . straight out of his face . . . those charges are going to be dropped." Rendell recalled the meeting. He remembered going out to the MOVE house to meet Delbert. However, he stated, "Delbert was talking nonsense. So I left."

Over the many months of negotiations, many exchanges like this may have taken place at which the parties talked past each other. In such unsupervised exchanges it is possible that one side could feel it made no agreement and the other might have felt it heard a significant concession being made. To avoid that ambiguity, mediators would do well to state specifically in the written agreement that there are no oral addenda.

However, it cannot be denied that it is difficult to write crystal-clear agreements, particularly in cases like this where saving face was a major concern. The city and its affiliate organizations needed to appear not to be giving in to pressure from their adversary. MOVE wanted to be seen as strong enough to standup to "the system." Perhaps in situations of this sort some have suggested that parties could sign a generalized written agreement that would be public record. Each party could save face by pointing to the ambiguous terms as supporting its position. They could also sign specific written protocols clarifying terms that would not be publicized. The protocols could be held in confidence at some agreed place, to be released only if a dispute arose over the interpretation of the agreement that had been made public. Not only would the second document leave a written record clarifying terms, but the threat of publicizing it in case of a violation might add further incentive for compliance.

This approach might work in some cases. However, it would be difficult in situations where one party is a government. It would no doubt create a problem of public trust if the city signed a confidential agreement which settled the dispute in a different manner than what the public was led to believe by the publicized document.

Another problem that may have caused difficulty with the May 5, 1978, agreement was the decision-making process within MOVE and the extent to which MOVE's negotiators could commit the rest of the members to an agreement. Intervenors had many different perceptions of the problem. Gaskins felt that Delbert Africa's team could bind MOVE. Other intervenors, however, felt that decisions had to be taken back and approved before they became binding, even though it was not clear what the approving body was. Some said the approval of the whole group was required, and others said only John Africa's approval was required.

Jerry Africa described MOVE's decision making as a consensus process. All members, not just those at the headquarters, had to approve a decision or it would not be binding on any. He added that this consensus extended beyond those physically present at the discussion. For instance, when Delbert Africa was negotiating an end to the blockade, Jerry Africa was in jail. Jerry held that since he did not approve of some of the terms of the agreement Delbert negotiated, the agreement was not binding on MOVE.

Interviews with many MOVE members confirm that MOVE's negotiators were limited in their ability to make binding agreements. Potential settlements had to be submitted to the group. Decisions were made by consensus, but John Africa's opinion was highly influential. Ramona Africa said that in these situations they would look to John Africa for guidance. He would point out things they had never seen. Because they had faith in him, they trusted his analysis. It is unclear, though, whether the group would automatically follow John Africa's lead or just give it great weight.

It would be useful for an intervenor to know the precise nature of this process. With that understanding the intervenor could either develop strategies to work with it, or might require that the party agree to a more flexible decision-making process as a condition for the intervention.

On the city's side, the district attorney made implementation more difficult when he changed his mind about the provision that kept MOVE away from the courts. This approach was bound to create difficulty even if it may not have been a clear violation of the ambiguous terms of the agreement. Requiring MOVE to appear in court, talking about the seriousness of the charges, and starting the trials during the 90-day truce period did not reassure MOVE that the city intended to terminate the conflict peacefully. On top of that, City Solicitor Albert added fuel to the fire when he declared that the city would tear the house down as soon as it was vacated.

Another problem may have arisen because not all the appropriate parties were represented in developing the agreement. Once the neighborhood, police, and city/court issues merged, intervenors did not include the neighborhood in their deliberations. They seem to have disregarded the fact that the neighbors' complaints were the source of the problem.

The effect of leaving the neighbors out was that the city adopted the most extreme position publicly taken by one neighborhood faction as a nonnegotiable item. That was PEHRC's initial demand that MOVE be removed from the area. As PEHRC was not represented in the negotiations, it could not modify the demand, and the position was treated as a fixed parameter. Had the neighborhood been represented in the negotiations, might a settlement have evolved that would not have required MOVE's evacuation? Might they have explored terms requiring strict compliance with health codes and basic standards of courtesy as a condition for MOVE remaining in the house?

The police were also left out of the peacemaking process. There was no observable effort to alter the relationship between MOVE and the rank-and-file police. The intervenors may have assumed that by dealing with the conflict at the top administrative level, the personal animosities between the police officers and MOVE would disappear. This was not the case. In fact, rank-and-file police were dissatisfied with the agreement because they considered it to be too soft on MOVE.[20] Their unresolved feelings of hostility may have played a major role in escalating the violence in the 1985 event. This experience suggests that in community conflicts where everyday interaction between the parties is inevitable, it is important to work toward reconciliation at the personal level to prevent implementation of the overall agreement from being sabotaged.*

*David Fattah suggested a program that could have been used to reduce police tensions in 1978. "A retreat should have been scheduled . . . for a counseling session with all police involved. Police should have been made to understand the danger of perpetrating a vendetta against organizations in Philadelphia." Could community groups have designed similar workshops for MOVE?

Another problem may have been the respective parties' differing views about the nature of the conflict. MOVE saw itself as a revolutionary political movement. It characterized its conflict with the neighbors and the city as a philosophical and political struggle, and referred to the jailed MOVE members as political prisoners. The CCCHR reinforced MOVE's claim that it was a political struggle by framing the conflict in terms of "human rights violations of blacks."

The city, on the other hand, responded with traditional police procedures that were derived from their experience in dealing with criminals. Unlike a criminal group, which might respond to punishment and deterrence, a group that sees itself as a revolutionary political movement might even be strengthened. It could attract more publicity, and galvanize sympathy and support from confrontation and challenge. The conflict itself might have a payoff. Therefore, traditional police techniques might be counterproductive with a group that sees itself as political.

The role of the media was another complicating factor. They seem to have played an exacerbating but at the same time a restraining role. Both city and MOVE supporters thought the press was biased against their cause. City Solicitor Sheldon Albert commented that police-community relations were no worse under the Rizzo administration than in other major cities at the time, but the press generated that perception. "Newspapers lie a lot. They do it all the time. [They] exaggerate."

MOVE members, on the other hand, repeatedly complained of biased coverage. They accused the press of portraying them as violent, filthy, and terroristic. They mentioned an instance where they were accused of eating dogs while in actuality they were basically vegetarians. They complained that neighbors who opposed them received media attention while those who either supported or tolerated them were ignored.

Furthermore, broad press coverage of the negotiations encouraged the parties to talk past each other in their attempt to impress the public about the justifiability of their respective positions. The public posturing may have limited the available options. One example is the issue of the release of the prisoners. This issue would not have been so thorny had it not been for the publicity. As Todd pointed out, "MOVE wanted to show that it could point a gun at the head of the city and get its demands met," which was part of its attempt to prove to everybody that it did not recognize the legitimacy of the legal system.

The city, on the other hand, had to publicly defend the integrity of the legal system, even though some officials privately conceded that the charges were trivial. Furthermore, Todd pointed out the various difficulties that arose because of inaccurate, inflammatory, or sensational reporting that heightened fear and suspicion between the parties. He attributed the failure of his attempt mainly to the "carnival atmosphere" created by the media.

On the other hand, the media focus on the conflict at times may have restrained the parties from using force. In fact, one reason MOVE members gave for their reluctance to relocate to the countryside was their fear of violence by their opponents if they were out of the vision of the press and the public. A MOVE pamphlet stated, "MOVE did not accept the farm because it was a trick the government was trying to use to get MOVE isolated so that they could kill us without witnesses."

From the above analysis, it seems clear that the reasons for the failure of the May 5 Agreement and the 1978 confrontation were a complex chain of actions and interactions. However, many people including the media adopted a simpler view that the 1978 confrontation took place solely because MOVE backed down on its agreement. This view, as will be shown later, might have contributed to a worse confrontation in 1985.

NOTES

1. "MOVE Bars Attendance at Hearings," *The Bulletin*, Mar. 16, 1978.

2. "Halting the Cult: A 10 Year Battle," *Philadelphia Daily News*, May 13, 1985, p. 7.

3. Interview with Ishongo Africa, *Philadelphia Inquirer*, Apr. 19, 1978, p. A1.

4. Karen Ditko, "Citywide Coalition Organized to Settle MOVE Encounter," *Philadelphia Tribune*, Mar. 14, 1978, pp. 1, 17.

5. Ibid.

6. Friendly Presence, "Religious Vigil: An Appeal to the People of Philadelphia," n.d. (Mimeographed.)

7. Forrest Black, "City Rejects State Help on MOVE Standoff," *Sunday Bulletin*, Apr. 2, 1978, p. 23.

8. CCCHR, "Resolution of Conflict in Powelton Village," n.d., p. 1. (Mimeographed.)

9. Ibid.

10. Andrew Wallace, "A Dispute Imperils MOVE Truce," *Philadelphia Inquirer*, May 24, 1978, p. C2.

11. Ibid.

12. Ibid.

13. "MOVE Has Virginia Branch," *Philadelphia Daily News*, Mar. 7, 1978, p. 4.

14. Sharon Sims Cox, as told to Carol Saline, "My Life with MOVE," *Philadelphia Magazine*, Sept. 1985, p. 240.

15. MOVE women, Untitled documented beginning, "Since the May 13th bombing . . . ," apparently written by MOVE women imprisoned in State Correctional Institute, Muncy, PA, 1986(?).

16. Phillip Weiss, "How He Bombed in Philadelphia: Goode, Bad, and Ugly." *The New Republic*, June 10, 1985, p. 12.

17. Thomas Kochman, *Black and White Styles in Conflict* (Chicago: University of Chicago Press, 1981), ch. 3.

18. Laura Blackburne, "A Framework for Analyzing the MOVE Conflict," *Conflict Resolution Notes* 4, no. 2 (Sept. 1986): 12.

19. Christopher Mitchell, "Six Puzzles About Community Conflicts: The MOVE Situation," *Conflict Resolution Notes*, 4, no. 2 (Sept. 1986): 16.

20. Murray Dubin and Robert Terry, "MOVE & City Reach Pact: Group to Give up Today," *Philadelphia Inquirer*, May 4, 1978, p. 1A.

PART 2
OSAGE, 1985

7

The Road to Osage Begins in Powelton

BEGINNINGS

The roots of the Osage Avenue conflict lie in Powelton Village. Six days after Judge DiBona's order to arrest the MOVE members in Powelton, 300 police officers and fire fighters arrived at the MOVE house. A gun battle ensued and police officer James Ramp was killed. Four other officers, six fire fighters, two MOVE members, and three MOVE sympathizers were wounded. MOVE was overpowered and surrendered. Some officers were seen on television dragging Delbert Africa out by his hair, hitting and kicking him. Later that day city bulldozers razed the house.

Almost a year after the arrest, in May 1979, several MOVE members were put on trial, charged with murder, attempted murder, assault, and conspiracy. Twelve had been arrested after the shoot-out. One, Davita Johnson Africa, had already been freed. Two other members, Consuela and Sandra Davis Africa, were tried separately. The rest were tried together at MOVE's insistence, because they felt that the arguments of each defendant might be essential for the defense of the others.

As usual, MOVE members insisted on representing themselves. They argued that no court-appointed lawyer, who had not been on the scene, could understand their case well enough to defend them properly. The court appointed backup attorneys and instructed them to help the defendants as much as

Powelton Shoot-Out

Source: Bulletin/Temple University Photojournalism Collection

they could. However, there was little cooperation between the attorneys and the defendants.

The trial has been characterized as "raucous" and "one of the longest and costliest" in the history of the city's criminal court system.[1] For the first month the trial proceeded relatively smoothly. However, MOVE's outspoken style of defense began to heat up when the MOVE members cross-examined the prosecution witnesses. According to legal commentators, the trial judge gave MOVE representatives unusual latitude in presenting their case. However, his patience grew thin. At one point he warned that MOVE's unorthodox cross-examination " 'constituted attempted proselytization,' and when he warned the defendants to confine themselves to an appropriate scope of questioning, they reacted with a series of outbursts."[2]

The disruptions continued to the point where the judge ordered the defendants removed from the courtroom until they would promise to behave according to the rules. MOVE did not comply with this requirement and remained barred from the rest of the proceedings.

The defense now lay in the hands of the backup attorneys. They had the unenviable task of representing clients who had rejected their services and refused to cooperate with them. The backup lawyers felt unable to present an active defense, and the MOVE members refused to comply with the judge's conditions in order to take the stand in their own defense. Seven out of the nine attorneys rested immediately or announced that they would not call witnesses. Two conducted a defense and called 16 witnesses, 8 of whom testified that the first shots had not come from the MOVE house, but originated from a building on the west side of the headquarters. About 30 policemen had testified that the first bullet was shot from the basement of the MOVE house.[3] In their concluding remarks, the attorneys argued that the prosecution had not proved who fired the bullet that killed the police officer. Furthermore, they felt the key element of intent had not been established. Since the shooter had not been identified, the prosecution had not proved his or her intent. Therefore, one could not be convicted of conspiring with or encouraging a homicide without establishing intent. Another defense attorney argued that no evidence was presented that their clients even possessed a gun on the day of the shoot-out. Others tried to argue that since it was unclear who fired the first shot, MOVE might have fired back in self-defense.

On August 4, 1981, the nine MOVE members were convicted of third-degree murder. They were sentenced to prison terms of 30 to 100 years. The tenth MOVE member to be convicted, Consuela Africa, was sentenced to 10 to 20 years on February 22, 1982. The trial lasted 21 months and cost more than $400,000.[4]

Meanwhile, three policemen were charged with beating Delbert Africa just after his surrender at the August 8, 1978, shoot-out. On February 2, 1981, in a move that stunned many people, the trial judge acquitted them.

In an announcement that took both the defense attorney and the prosecutor by surprise, the judge ordered a directed verdict as the attorneys were preparing to make closing arguments to the jury. . . . The judge stated "Philadelphia is bleeding to death because of this MOVE tragedy. . . . No verdict from those good people from Dauphin County (the jurors) will staunch the flow of blood. . . . It can only be stopped by setting up a lightning rod. I will be that lightning rod.[5]

After the 1978 shoot-out, MOVE dropped from public view, but the Philadelphia political scene had been profoundly altered. Jim Quinn, writing in the *Village Voice,* observed, "MOVE seemed to disappear, and Rizzo claimed victory. But the outcry over his tactics helped finish Rizzo's career. He never won another election in Philadelphia.[6]

Frank Rizzo was succeeded by moderate Democrat Bill Green. Green's administration implemented long-neglected police procedures that were designed to reduce the chance of citizen deaths and harassment by the police. For instance, for the first time the Philadelphia police adopted a firearms policy that specifically defined the situations in which weapons could be used. The number of citizen complaints declined.

In the early 1980s George Fencl died. His replacement as head of the Civil Affairs Division of the Philadelphia Police Department did not have Fencl's clout. Wilson Goode became city manager under Mayor Green. In May 1980, Goode established a multifaceted crisis response mechanism to be supervised by his office. The program was called the City Intervention Program (CIP). City Manager Goode planned to handle community tensions by using CIP to coordinate the response of city agencies and city-funded crisis management programs. Its special responsibility was "[to intervene] in the immediate problem of gang related, youth, racial, and neighborhood incidents and create an appropriate environment for addressing the causes of the problem . . . [and to provide] an overall policy and working coordination among the [involved] agencies in *crisis situations*. [emphasis added][7]

The City Intervention Program (CIP) was to coordinate the Police Department, Welfare Department, the Crisis Intervention Network (CIN), the Human Relations Commission, the Community Intervention Program, and the Managing Director's Office. Other city agencies and services, such as the Department of Licenses and Inspection and the Health Department, were to be involved as situations required.

Some of the agencies under the program had considerable experience in dealing with community tensions. The Crisis Intervention Network originally worked with gang violence. Its mission later evolved toward handling racial and religious violence in schools. The Community Intervention Program was set up to decrease racial tension and juvenile crime. The Human Relations Commission was established primarily to administer and enforce anti-discrimination ordinances. It had a Community Service Division that mediated neighborhood disputes referred by the district attorney. The Human Relations Commission also provided prevention and intervention services in situations of community tension and interracial or intergroup problems. The Civil Affairs Bureau of the Philadelphia Police Department specialized in interracial and intergroup conflicts.

The participating members of CIP were to meet every week to share information and coordinate their plans. Under Wilson Goode's directive the managing director could determine whether to declare a situation "critical." If he did so, his liaison, a ranking police official, and the executive director of the Crisis

Intervention Network would form a team to coordinate the response. The CIP's executive director would assume full direction of the civilian intervention workers until the crisis was over.

After implementing this plan, Goode ran for mayor and won. When he was inaugurated in January 1984, he became the first black to hold Philadelphia's highest office. He had strong black and liberal white backing, and quickly established a reputation as a mayor who got things done.

However, the CIP he had established as city manager fell into disrepair during his campaign. During his administration, although the agencies still met weekly in the City Manager's Office, city officials seldom called on it or outside agencies to attend to troublesome situations in Philadelphia neighborhoods. For instance, Clarence Farmer, executive director of Philadelphia's Commission on Human Relations, recalled that under the Rizzo administration he was routinely called on to defuse troubled situations in order to avoid police action. The Goode administration, however, seldom consulted with his office.

Philadelphia's leadership had changed in the years that MOVE was out of the news. None in the new leadership had had direct experience with MOVE in 1978 except District Attorney Ed Rendell, who by then was preoccupied with plans for running for governor.

MOVE REAPPEARS

In the early 1980s, during the Bill Green administration, MOVE members began to reappear. Some of them were extradited by the city of Philadelphia from Rochester, New York, and other areas to which they had dispersed after the 1978 shoot-out. They were brought back on outstanding warrants arising from the May 20, 1977, confrontation. In 1981 a few members and children of the imprisoned MOVE members moved into 6221 Osage Avenue, a house belonging to Louise James, John Africa's sister. Later, some other adult members joined them.

Initially there was little tension between MOVE and the Osage Avenue residents. In fact, some neighbors stated that they did not even realize that MOVE members were living there. According to Larry Rawls of the CIN, Osage Avenue residents were sympathetic to MOVE's situation during the 1978 blockade and had been involved in supplying food to them. One Osage resident stated, "We welcomed them, and their children played with our children. . . . We [even] purchased winter coats for their children."[8] Other neighbors pointed out that they had fed MOVE children.

People had different theories about why MOVE members started living on Osage Avenue. Bennie Swans of the CIN believed that they had planned a confrontation with the city from the beginning, and moved to Osage Avenue with this challenge in mind. It was a middle-class neighborhood they could push around. A lower-class neighborhood would not have allowed itself to be harassed in the way that Swans felt MOVE planned to do. Jerry Africa claimed that there was no particular motive for moving to Osage except that the members did not have any place to live, and John Africa's sister made her house available to them.

After the initial peaceful period, a life-style conflict began to emerge, similar to the one in Powelton. Neighbors complained that MOVE children were rooting in their trash for food and appeared to be hungry. Problems such as leaving garbage outside, collecting animals and giving them raw meat, cutting flea collars off neighbors' pets, and feeding pigeons and building coops for them created friction between MOVE and its neighbors. The Osage residents complained to city officials. One neighbor stated, "At first, I complained directly to them [MOVE] about trash and garbage laid on our property. . . . They were cooperative. They would say OK and they would move things. . . . But as time went on, conditions just grew continuously worse."[9] By October 1983, neighbors also started complaining of MOVE's verbal harassment.

They petitioned several city departments and met with politicians, city, and police officials. All appeared to be reluctant to act. However, plainclothes officers maintained a regular presence. On October 19, 1983, Osage neighbors met with State Representative Peter Truman to seek help. However, they were persuaded to delay pressing for action until after the upcoming mayoral election, in order "not to jeopardize Wilson Goode's election chances." [10]

Clarence Farmer, who was still director of the Commission on Human Relations, recalled intervening in one neighborhood conflict. The MOVE house was in the middle of a block of row houses. Access to garages was through a back alley. Suddenly, without consulting the neighbors, MOVE fenced off the alley behind its house for a dog run. Neighbors were incensed because they had been cut off from their garages. Farmer heard about the problem from his staff person, Gloria Sutton, who was still maintaining contact with MOVE.

Farmer arranged for a meeting with MOVE. Two or three members came to his office and met for two and a half hours. Ramona Africa later summarized MOVE's position. She said that they did not deny access to anyone when they blocked the alley. Neighbors could reach their garages from either end of the block, and no one ever used the alley anyway. She added that after the controversy died down, a policeman who lived up the alley built a cinder block wall across the alley and nobody complained. Farmer, however, convinced them that their action was a violation of the neighbors' rights to free access and that MOVE would be getting into trouble. City agencies would have to come in and tear the fence down. MOVE agreed to remove it. However, "two weeks later," Farmer said, "it was back up again. This time they had a wall with a bell on it. If people wanted to go through, they had to ring a bell, and MOVE would open the gate." Farmer told them that was not satisfactory, but before he could follow up on it, he was removed from office to make way for an appointee of the new administration.

On another front, since their return, MOVE members had been writing to public officials, and trying to meet city and federal authorities to press for the release of their colleagues who were serving time on the 1978 charges. Jerry Africa, who along with Ramona Africa held the title of MOVE's minister of information, said that he was attempting to get a hearing for MOVE's demands. He approached various people on the basis of what he felt were incontestable and glaring legal irregularities in the 1978 criminal proceedings. He argued that all the evidence showed a deliberate and preplanned attempt by the city to suppress MOVE. Some of the points he made were the following:

1. Under Pennsylvania's speedy trial law, trial must be commenced within 180 days of arrest or charges must be dismissed. Some of the cases violated this rule.
2. Judge DiBona's contempt citation, which precipitated the 1978 shootout, was illegal because it was the city rather than MOVE that broke the May 5 agreement.
3. Judge DiBona, who presided over civil court, had no authority to issue warrants on some of the criminal matters involved.
4. The arrest under Judge DiBona's warrant was illegal. Hence MOVE's resistance was an act of self-defense.

Other arguments MOVE members raised were that they did not kill the police officer. They said he was struck by a stray bullet fired by the other police officers. Delbert Africa maintained that there was testimony in the trial that Officer Ramp was shot from behind. The wound in the front of his neck was an exit wound. However, he added, this testimony was changed later in order to make it appear that MOVE shot Ramp from the front. He added that the City demolished the MOVE headquarters immediately after the shoot-out, so that the trajectory of the bullets could not be shown. Moreover, MOVE contended that even if it were proved to be a MOVE bullet, it was unjust to sentence nine people to 30-100 years in prison when only one could have shot the officer.

After returning from Rochester in 1981, Jerry Africa said he met with Managing Director Wilson Goode and documented these legal problems for him. Jerry stated that Goode promised to arrange a meeting for him with District Attorney Ed Rendell to review the legal questions, but the session never took place. Jerry explained the city's reluctance to get a hearing for MOVE's grievances by saying, "The city was trapped in its position. For it to agree with our analysis would require it to admit to a monumental series of mistakes or wrongdoings which would end Rendell's political career."

Ed Rendell disagreed with Jerry Africa's analysis. "[The judge] did a superb job. He bent over backwards. Almost every procedural and evidentiary break was given the MOVE defendants. His verdict was a compromise verdict. The evidence was ample for first degree murder."

Louise James testified that she talked with Wilson Goode after he became mayor, but

The Mayor doesn't say too much. He listens. . . . He was saying that he couldn't do anything, about the problem. He would look into the matter. . . . He said he would contact Governor Thornburgh and possibly see what he could do, if anything about the people at least getting a pardon, or, at least, some one looking into MOVE being incarcerated. . . . [11]

However, nothing came of this meeting.

Delbert Africa pointed out that the district attorney and the courts were persecuting the MOVE organization rather than prosecuting them for the crimes MOVE members committed. He and Ramona Africa noted that on several occasions, MOVE members were told that their charges would be dropped if they renounced their MOVE membership. They claimed that those who did so were not charged. They referred to Lee Sing, Sharon Penn, and Lamont Gaskins, who had been charged with offenses arising from the May 20, 1977, confrontation "but told the judge that they were no longer MOVE members, and that they do not follow John Africa. They let them go. On the other hand, Sue Africa, who refused to make such a declaration, is still in prison."

Delbert Africa also indicated that Sandra Davis was in the MOVE house during the 1978 shoot-out along with the other people who were convicted of conspiracy to kill the policeman. However, she was let go because she was not a MOVE member. He contended, "We wasn't supposed to be charged nor convicted of being MOVE members. We were supposed to be convicted of committing crimes. If they can drop the charges at will for others, there is no reason they cannot release us."

Jerry Africa returned to prison to serve the remainder of his original sentence.* After ten months he was released on parole, and continued talking to "anyone who might have influence."

---

*This was on the charges for which he had been released on appeal bond in the compromise that led to the 1978 settlement.

He said he tried to reach black city councilmen, judges, and the district attorney. He also spent time talking with Clarence Farmer of the Philadelphia Human Relations Commission.

Farmer's policy was to maintain an open door to hear MOVE out. Jerry and other MOVE members came to his office to ask him to help them find ways to gain the release of their imprisoned members. Farmer said he told them, " 'I don't know how to do that. That is in court. It can only be done through the judicial process.' They had no other alternative." At one time they told him their plans to picket City Hall. "I talked them out of that," recalls Farmer. "I said, 'All you will do is to embarrass yourselves. You don't have enough sympathizers to make it impressive. That was ineffective.' So they passed it up."

At this point, it seems there was confusion in the minds of many about exactly what MOVE's demands were and whether they were negotiable. Most, like Farmer, felt that MOVE wanted outright release of all its prisoners. They saw this as an unrealistic demand. Father Paul Washington, a close confidant of the mayor and a person who had experience mediating with MOVE in 1978, saw it as "an impossible demand. I cannot think there would be any conditions under which [that could happen]. Well, they were tried in court and found guilty and sentenced. How can you arrest that? That is why I felt it was impossible."

Lary Groth, deputy director of the Commission on Human Relations, said that MOVE wanted an immediate and unconditional release of its members, which was impossible and irrational. Because of this, Groth said, he and Farmer advised the mayor to prepare for a confrontation.

Bennie Swans of the CIN, however, suggested that MOVE was after a process to review the irregularities of the charges and trials. Phil Africa supported Swan's analysis. "All we were trying to do was to get people to put pressure on the city of Philadelphia not to release us, but to honestly investigate the facts. An honest investigation would lead to no other outcome but our release."

ESCALATION ON OSAGE AVENUE

In late 1983, the tensions at Osage Avenue began to escalate. Referring to Christmas Eve, one neighbor said:

One minute after midnight, MOVE nailed up their house with boards. We heard the noise . . . and looked outside. There were all the neighbors looking out too. Little children says, "What is it? Is it Santy Clause?" Then MOVE started on that bullhorn, and the first thing they said was " . . . MF Santy Claus, MF Santy Claus." Can you imagine the face on those little children? MF Santy Claus. It went on all night, and every night from there.[12]

There are various opinions about why MOVE started haranguing the Osage neighbors. The first and simplest one is that MOVE never respected the system. Using obscenities was a part of its shock strategy to show its lack of respect, and the harangue was a continuation of this behavior. Others ascribe a more complicated interpretation. Bennie Swans pointed out that it was a bargaining ploy to get the city to respond to MOVE's plight. Nobody was paying attention to its demands to release its imprisoned members. If MOVE were to seriously inconvenience a middle-class neighborhood, which might have some influence with the city, then the city would come under pressure to come to terms with MOVE.

Jerry Africa's interpretation confirmed this analysis:

So finally, after being frustrated with all my attempts [to negotiate], the people at Osage Avenue decided to get into a confrontation. They gave me some time. They said, "Listen Jerry, we'll do it that way, but if it don't work, we'll have to do it our way." And that is what May 13, 1985, is about. Not that that particular day was the day we had chosen to actually confront. They was still in the process—they were going to let that thing drag out. Really, they didn't want to come to a confrontation. They just wanted the publicity and exposure to get attention focused on this. We know the politicians respond to the public. We wanted to let people know what we perceived.

Delbert Africa recalled:

Our people were telling them [the Osage neighbors], "All the complaints that you got, why don't you take them to the city? Tell them the reason MOVE is doing it is because they want their people home." The reason our people were doing this is because they couldn't get Wilson Goode to listen.

He added that they did try to accommodate the neighbors somewhat.

When the bullhorn heated up, and the people were coming up with complaints about being kept up all night, our people [changed their practice. Instead of using the bullhorn] all night, twenty-four hours a day, we was just going to run it during the day. That was done, and it was shown. It gradually got to the point where it wasn't done at all.

As the haranguing started, the neighbors called the police. However, the city appeared to be avoiding a confrontation by doing as little as possible. The police responded by monitoring the situation from the street. On April 13, 1984, MOVE members "harassed" a City Water Department crew as it was trying to shut off MOVE's water for unpaid bills. Plainclothes police monitoring the neighborhood stopped the crew from turning off the water. In another example, the State Parole Board had declared Frank James Africa "delinquent" for failure to report to his probation officer, and issued a warrant for his arrest. The police are reported to have refused to arrest, citing the sensitive situation. On May 3, 1984, neighbors complained that a masked man with a shotgun was on the roof of MOVE's house. Police temporarily evacuated the neighbors while more than 40 policemen surrounded the MOVE residence. The standoff lasted about an hour and a half, and ended without casualties. No further action was taken. Between May 13 and 27, MOVE staged a series of weekend loudspeaker addresses to the community and threatened public officials.

Bennie Swans of the CIN intervened at this stage to see if it would be possible to mediate this situation. He sought authorization from the city managing director to start negotiation. However, he was told that "The vehicle [that the managing director would use] to resolve the problem with MOVE was the police, [and] that at this particular point, all further civilian interaction was to cease, and it was in fact a police matter."[13]

On May 13, 1984, as problems were mounting, neighbors met with MOVE. Swan described the meeting thus:

MOVE initiated it by calling out over their loudspeakers for the neighbors to come out and talk. They only succeeded in talking past each other. The neighbors challenged MOVE about boarding up their house. [They complained that] it was affecting their property values, and the loudspeaker was intolerable.

MOVE stated their position. "People are unjustly detained in prison. They are black people, and you are black too. Why aren't you raising hell for their release?" The meeting never moved beyond position-taking. "They were actually saying to the neighbors, 'We need your help. Now you can do that willingly or unwillingly, but nevertheless, you are going to help us.'"

Jerry Africa defended MOVE's use of the bullhorn. To him it was just a communications device. "When there were some issues where the community was challenging our organization or our organization's position, we felt there was a need to respond to it. Once that thing was addressed, that was it."

The neighbors continued to approach Mayor Goode, demanding that something be done. The mayor's response was that he had no legal basis for evicting MOVE. Violations of the city's sanitation codes were summary offenses. The law allowed the authorities only to issue summonses to appear in court. Nobody wanted MOVE people in court again, since they would turn it into a circus. The mayor assured the neighbors that he was searching for a permanent legal solution. In the meantime he offered a mental health counseling program for children traumatized by MOVE harassment.

On May 30, 1984, the mayor, managing director, police commissioner, city solicitor, and district attorney met with a U.S. attorney plus some officials of the FBI and the Secret Service, and were told that no grounds existed for federal action against MOVE. The U.S. attorney cautioned city officials not to violate the civil rights of the occupants of the MOVE house. In the meantime, the police commissioner instructed a sergeant to prepare a plan to remove MOVE from the house. On July 22, 1984, the district attorney advised the mayor that legal grounds existed for arresting some of the residents of the MOVE house. However, the mayor decided not to take immediate action. Instead, he would wait and see what would occur on August 8, the sixth anniversary of the Powelton shoot-out. On July 31, Louise James, John Africa's sister, and her niece, Laverne Sims reportedly told the mayor that MOVE members were becoming more desperate and were prepared to use weapons.

On August 8, 1984, there were rumors that MOVE might incite a violent confrontation. Hundreds of police surrounded the block. MOVE used its bullhorn to taunt the officers. The stakeout ended with no incidents, except for a cherry bomb that a child tossed into the street.

Responding to another demand from the neighbors, the Mayor stated that he would act when he decided it would be appropriate. In the fall of 1984 and winter of 1985, MOVE members started fortifying their residence and built a bunker on their roof. Neighbors and plainclothes police saw MOVE members taking tree trunks, steel sheeting, and lumber into the house, but the loudspeakers were silent. Neighbors reported that the harassment declined. Swans assumed that MOVE members were so busy fortifying the house that they did not have time to harass the neighbors. However, later in the spring, they resumed the bullhorn harangues. On April 29, neighbors and police surveillance officers listened as MOVE members threatened to kill the mayor and any police that would dare come in the MOVE residence. MOVE also warned that it had wired the block with explosives. In addition, neighbors told the police that they had seen men with rifles in the bunker on the rooftop. Soon after, the neighbors held a press conference to complain that the city had consistently ignored their grievances. They threatened to take the matter into their own hands, and asked the governor and attorney general for help.

Events began accelerating in May 1985. On May 2, neighbors reported that they saw a five-gallon gasoline can hoisted to the MOVE rooftop. On May 3, the mayor concluded that an armed conflict between MOVE and the neighbors was a probability and ordered the district attorney to reexamine the legal grounds for the city taking action against MOVE. The police and prosecutors interviewed 19 residents to support an application for search and arrest warrants on firearms charges.

On May 7, 1985, the mayor met with the city's managing director, police commissioner, and district attorney. At this meeting, he authorized the police commissioner to prepare and execute a tactical plan to evict MOVE and arrest some of its members on misdemeanor charges. The police commissioner was to be supervised by the managing director. The police commissioner then delegated the planning to three officers: the head of the Bomb Disposal Unit, a sergeant from the pistol range, and a uniformed patrolman. Later investigations revealed that the planners lacked sufficient expertise for a task of this sort.[14]

Mayor Goode later testified that he had ordered that all the children in the MOVE house must be taken out before any action was to be taken, and that none of the police officers involved in the 1978 Powelton shoot-out should participate in this eviction plan. His concern was that these officers might have residual anger from the 1978 conflict and might act on it. By May 9, the three officers had developed their tactical plan with no supervision from the police commissioner or the managing director. On May 9, the managing director left town on personal business and did not return until the evening of May 12. On May 11, city officials obtained search and arrest warrants from the court to be served on the MOVE members.

On May 12, before the managing director returned, the police commissioner briefed the mayor about the plan. The mayor approved it and authorized its execution for the morning of May 13. On May 12 police evacuated all MOVE's Osage Avenue neighbors. However, they did not prevent the MOVE children from returning to the MOVE house when they came back from their daily exercise in the park.

On May 13 at 3:00 A.M., police placed a bomb disposal and stakeout unit in a parking lot near Osage Avenue. Contrary to the mayor's alleged order, several police officers who took part in the 1978 shoot-out were present among the assault force. The police commissioner and tactical planners held a general briefing inside an on-site command center and then cut off gas and electricity to the entire neighborhood. The fire department positioned high-pressure water hoses.

At 5:35 A.M. the police commissioner announced over a bullhorn that 4 people inside MOVE's house were named in arrest warrants and had 15 minutes to surrender. MOVE used its loudspeaker to broadcast its refusal. At 5:50 A.M. police fired tear gas and smoke projectiles to provide cover for police insertion teams while they entered two houses on the left and the right of the MOVE headquarters. At the same time, the first shots were fired at police from the MOVE house.

Police opened fire on the house, and in the next 90 minutes shot at least 10,000 rounds of ammunition. The assault was backed with additional stores of ammunition, machine guns, antitank weapons, and explosives. Insertion teams detonated explosives to blow holes in the walls to insert tear gas. By 10:40 A.M. the front of the house was blown out, but the reinforcements MOVE had installed prevented police from dislodging those inside.

By 12:30 P.M. it became clear that these tactics had failed. Around 3:45, Mayor Goode said in a televised press conference that he intended to seize control of the house by any means necessary. Meanwhile, police debated using other kinds of explosives.

At 4:30 the police commissioner, in the presence of the managing director, instructed the head of the Bomb Disposal Unit to assemble an explosive package to dislodge the bunker that MOVE had constructed on top of their house. It would be dropped from a helicopter. The managing director advised the mayor of the plan by 4:45, and very shortly thereafter, Mayor Goode approved it. At 5:27 P.M. the bomb was dropped. It failed to dislodge the bunker immediately, but it ignited the gasoline tank and started a fire. The police and fire commissioners let the bunker burn. The flames quickly engulfed the house and spread to the neighboring homes. At 6:32 P.M. the fire department turned its hoses on the fire for the first time. But it was not until around 9:30 P.M. that they took more active steps to fight it. By that time, the flames were burning out of control and were not contained until 11:41 P.M. By then nearly two square blocks of residential neighborhood had been burned. Fire destroyed 61 homes, damaged 110 others, and killed 11 occupants of the MOVE home, 5 of them children. Some 250 men, women, and children were left homeless. Of those in MOVE's house, only one woman and one child survived: Ramona and Birdie Africa.

After the crisis, the mayor established a special 11-person commission to investigate the crisis and present recommenda-

Fire at Osage Avenue

Source: Philadelphia Daily News Photo Department. Reprinted with permission

Source: Philadelphia Daily News Photo Department. Reprinted with permission

tions. Some of its findings were that the arrest warrants were only for four residents in the house, and the rest of the occupants had no outstanding warrants or charges. It also found that once the house was on fire some members and children tried to escape from the building, but were prevented by police gunfire. In its conclusion, the report stated*:

The Commission believes that the decision of various city officials to permit construction of the bunker, to allow the use of high explosives and, in a 90 minute period, the firing of at least 10,000 rounds of ammunition at the house, to sanction the dropping of a bomb on an occupied row house, and to let a fire burn in a row house occupied by children, would not likely have been made had the MOVE house and its occupants been situated in a comparable white neighborhood.[15]

The Commission characterized city officials' behavior as follows:

The Mayor's failure to call a halt to the operation on May 12th when he knew that children were in the house, was grossly negligent. . . . [16]
The Managing Director and Police Commissioner were grossly negligent and clearly risked the lives of the children by failing to take effective steps to detain them. . . . [17]
The Mayor abdicated his responsibilities as a leader. . . . [18]
The plan to bomb the MOVE house was reckless, ill-conceived and hastily approved.[19]
The hasty, reckless and irresponsible decision by the Police Commissioner and the Fire Commissioner to use the fire as a tactical weapon was unconscionable.[20]

Among other things, the Commission recommended that the decisions and actions of all concerned city officials be fully investigated by the District Attorney and the United States Department of Justice.[21]

*Former Pennsylvania Supreme Court Justice Bruce Kaufmann, who was a member of the Commission, disagreed with some of the views of the majority, and wrote a dissenting view in a separate report.

NOTES

1. Murray Dubin, "Revolution Ain't Verbalized . . . ," *Philadelphia Inquirer,* May 9, 1980, p. A14.

2. Linda Traver Pirolli, "Litigation History of MOVE: The Judicial System on Trial," *Philadelphia Law Journal.* Sept. 22, 1980, p. 6.

3. Dubin, "Revolution Ain't Verbalized . . . ," p. A14.

4. Ibid.

5. Jan Schaffer, "Judge Acquits Policemen in Beating Before MOVE Case Goes to Jury," *Philadelphia Inquirer,* Feb. 3, 1981. p. A1.

6. Jim Quinn, "They Bombed in West Philly," *Village Voice,* May 28, 1985, p. 1: see also Phillip Weiss,"How He Bombed in Philadelphia: Goode, Bad, and Ugly," *The New Republic,* June 10, 1985, p. 12.

7. Committee on Community Tensions of the Fellowship Commission, "City Response to Intergroup Violence," December, 1983, p. 5. Mimeographed.

8. Transcript of the Philadelphia Special Commission to Investigate the MOVE Crisis, *Philadelphia Inquirer,* Oct. 28, 1985, Special Section, p. 3-C.

9. Ibid.

10. "The Bombing of West Philly," *Frontline,* Public Television Service Documentary, May 6, 1987. Transcribed by the authors.

11. Transcript, Special Commission, p. 5-C.

12. Quinn, "They Bombed in West Philly," p. 1.

13. Transcript, Special Commission, p. 5-C.

14. "The Findings, Conclusions and Recommendations of the Philadelphia Special Investigation Commission," March 6, 1986, p. 31. (Mimeographed.)

15. Ibid.

16. "Findings . . . ," Finding no. 15.

17. "Findings . . . ," Finding no. 16.

18. "Findings . . . ," Finding no. 22.

19. "Findings . . . ," Finding no. 24.

20. "Findings . . . ," Finding no. 27.

21. "Findings . . . ," Recommendation no. 38.

8
Crisis Intervention

As the events spiraled toward their fiery conclusion in May 1985, a few people were involved in frantic efforts to ward off disaster. The following were some of the most visible attempts at bringing a peaceful settlement to this conflict.

CRISIS INTERVENTION NETWORK

One of the few organized attempts at an early intervention in the conflict was by the Crisis Intervention Network. CIN was established as a city agency in 1975 and was charged with defusing gang violence, a serious problem in Philadelphia at the time. Bennie Swans, CIN's director, pointed out that the Network was cut from the city in 1978 because of its role in trying to bring in federal and state agencies to mediate the first MOVE conflict. After considerable bargaining a political compromise was found in which the agency was reorganized as a nonprofit agency but received 98 percent of its funds from the city. Its mandate broadened as the gang problem began to abate, and by the 1980s it worked on general community tensions.

Swans recounted that in May 1984, Osage neighbors were complaining about the MOVE members jogging on neighboring rooftops, and the noise and profanity coming out of the bullhorn. Further, a fistfight broke out between two youths, one from MOVE and the other a neighbor. Soon the fathers got drawn into the fight. Tensions spread throughout the neighborhood. The Civil Affairs Division of the Philadelphia Police Department asked CIN to intervene.

Swans put together a team of staff members with close connections to MOVE. Bob Owens, Swans's assistant, for instance, had grown up with some MOVE members, and knew Conrad and Jerry Africa well. Swans said, "I identified five staff persons that had a history of being effective in working with progressive political organizations."[1] He felt MOVE could best be understood in terms of its "progressive, revolutionary organizing" roots.

The CIN staff talked to MOVE members and the neighbors. They learned from MOVE that the conflict involved more than life-style. When asked why they were alienating the neighbors, "[MOVE's] response was clear—that through the alienation of the residents, [they could] bring the city to the point of confrontation or compromise as it related to the release of the persons arrested, unfairly in their view, in the 1978 shootout."[2]

Swans testified that MOVE sought a fair procedure for reviewing its case. He referred to a conversation with one of MOVE's Osage Avenue spokespersons, Conrad Africa. "Conrad alluded to a process . . . something that would begin to review the charges of conspiracy that they felt were trumped up against their members; that that would be sufficient to begin to break the impasse."

He learned from the neighbors that the situation was explosive. The neighbors told him that they were feeling helpless and had no one to turn to, that they thought about taking the situation in their own hands. Although the city did little to resolve the problem, it promised it would. He felt that "Since middle-class families tend to trust the system, the neighbors had faith that the city would take care of their problem." Unlike Powelton, where there were pro- and anti-MOVE groups, the only groups organizing in Osage Avenue were in opposition to MOVE and oriented toward involving the city in resolving the problem.

Swans's analysis was that through their rhetoric and actions, MOVE had challenged the neighborhood men's sense of manhood.

There were these black men who for such a very long time were pur-
chasing their homes, going to be run out of their neighborhood. Their
family members were saying, "You going to let these people run you
out of your house, let them insult your family, disrespect your wife,
your children?" Manhood becomes a very important issue for minori-
ties—blacks and Hispanics. Manhood is often the only thing that one
has, and that was being threatened by the existence of the MOVE
organization.

Swans both listened to and challenged both sides' positions.
He appealed to neighbors: "What will you gain from a violent
confrontation?" His approach to MOVE was to get them to re-
think their tactics. He pointed out to them that their present
tactics were only

. . . alienating their support base; [and] that it made no sense for an
organization that was political in nature to alienate their support base
. . . that many of the residents and neighbors in that area had, in fact,
been persons that had brought food to their barricaded area in Powelton Village; that the persons were not insensitive to them, as other
black persons that were caught up in the struggle.[3]

He suggested that MOVE adopt different tactics that could
encourage the neighbors to support MOVE's concerns. The
tactics would begin with negotiation on a resolvable issue: the
loudspeaker. Proceeding this way, MOVE could offer to aban-
don using other offensive practices if the neighbors would work
with MOVE in getting their prisoners released.

Swans did not pursue this negotiation strategy because he
felt he needed city approval to become involved. He reasoned
that the city was both a party and the primary source of his
funding. He was mindful that his agency was almost destroyed
for its role in the 1978 conflict and was hesitant to risk its destruction again. Swans relayed his findings and his recommendation that negotiation should continue to Mayor Goode. Apparently the mayor never responded. Swans raised the matter
at one of the Tuesday meetings at the City Manager's Office,
where the city-related crisis intervention agencies were coordinated. He expressed his view that "negotiations begin with the

bullhorn as an entry point, in order to engage in more substantive discussions later."[4]

Swans recalled the city manager had a different view: "[He] indicated that he had reviewed the situation, that he had determined that the vehicle he would use to resolve the problem with MOVE was the police; that at this particular point all further civilian interaction was to cease and [it was] in fact, a police matter."[5]

Swans said that the city took the position that confrontation was inevitable. The city's primary concern then became how to prepare for it, how to acquire the necessary political support, and how to have a sufficient legal base to avoid criticism. From this point on, CIN staff maintained only informal contact with MOVE members and did not attempt any other intervention until the last minute.

MICHAEL A. NUTTER

Michael A. Nutter, a young black staff person for City Councilman Ortiz, and campaign manager for the Democratic candidate for district attorney, Judge Robert Williams, reported on his involvement.

About two weeks before the May 13 event, he talked to Ahmid Fareed, a community worker who had contacts with the mayor, about the mounting tensions on Osage Avenue. Nutter offered to help out. He said, "MOVE had said they pretty well didn't want to talk to any politicians or elected officials. They would only deal with grass-roots community people, and Fareed was a grass-roots type of person." Because Nutter worked for the city, he had access to city officials. He felt that technically he was not a politician, and so could communicate with MOVE. Neither Fareed nor the Mayor's Office followed up on this offer.

On Mothers' Day, Sunday, May 12, while on his way to visit his mother, who lived near the Osage area, Nutter saw the mounting police presence. He talked with some of his friends in the neighborhood who had grown up with many MOVE members. One was Charles Burrus, a community activist associated with the Inner-City Organizing Network, Inc., and a childhood friend of Jerry Africa. They told Nutter that they had already talked with the people in 6221 Osage and had not succeeded in getting them to come out of the house. Nutter and his friends brainstormed about some other tactics or questions to ask. They decided to go to the property to see MOVE.

Nutter and Burrus were allowed through the police lines because of Nutter's city identification card. Nutter described the encounter graphically.

We went down to the house, and Charles made what seems to be a greeting that you make when you come to the MOVE house. It's just like a saying or a statement. There was a little bell outside that looks like a pull string—a little cowbell. They had an enclosed porch with wood slats covering everything. They were interspersed so you couldn't really see in. Behind the wood was a burlap sack type of material, which because it was daytime you could see through. If you were standing behind it, I would not be able to see your face. . . . the person we were speaking to was Ramona, and they addressed her as Ramona or Mona. I identified myself and told her my name and told her that I was affiliated with the city. I didn't want to emphasize that I worked for the city or that I worked for a politician because I was concerned they would just say, "Leave, I don't want to talk to you."

It pretty much centered around Ramona, and somewhere else to the side of the porch were other people. You couldn't see them, but you knew they were there. Sometimes you would ask her a question, and you could see her head move to the side in the direction to get some advice or guidance from these people so as to give the right answer.

Basically, they outlined where they were, and we asked them questions—back and forth. We just said, "Why won't you come out of the house? The neighborhood is surrounded. It's been evacuated." Basically, the response was, "We don't have to come out of the house. We haven't done anything wrong. We aren't hurting anybody, and we're not going to leave. And we want our brothers and sisters who are illegally incarcerated in prison to come home. We want them released from prison."

Common sense and understanding of the judicial process tells you they weren't going to be released. They had had a trial, and according to our system, were duly convicted of murder. I tried to explain that to them. They said, "We don't agree with that. We're not going to leave, even if they come home."

Early on it had been said they would leave the house if MOVE members were released from prison. We tried to explore with them what it would take. Where along the line in the process would you be willing to leave the neighborhood or to resolve this problem? Would it take a new hearing? Would you have to have a new trial scheduled? Would it be enough to have the mayor, the district attorney, and the chief justice of the Pennsylvania Supreme Court to have a press conference and say "We are willing to take a look into this case again and retry it, or whatever?"

They said, "No, none of that. We would never trust them. We want them released, and even if they come home, we're not going to leave."

At that point I was firmly convinced that they were not going to leave the house under any circumstances. Then I just said, "Look, do you realize that the neighborhood is surrounded with police officers; that it is going to be fully evacuated by later tonight; and that more than likely, somewhere in the next 24 hours this house is going to be assaulted by police officers?"

Her response was very direct and very to the point. She said, "Yes, I understand that and we are prepared for them."

At that point I didn't see any further need for discussion. No one else had any questions, and didn't say anything, and we left.

Nutter evaluated his intervention thus:

I didn't necessarily believe that by me coming down the street and coming up to the house that they were just going to walk out. They didn't know me from the man in the moon. I tried to provide some access through which they could funnel some complaint or get back to the mayor or managing director and articulate some concerns and demands that they might have. As it got closer to the eleventh hour, sometimes people have a way of changing or realizing the severity of the situation.

This issue of the children [trying to get them removed from the house before the assault] I did not raise, because I'd been told by the people that had gone down earlier that they had asked them on a couple of occasions earlier that day to at least release the children. They'd been flatly turned down, and the response was that they would rather have their children die than turn them over to the system."

Novella Williams, a community activist, also narrated her involvement:

They had barricaded the whole area, up and down Osage. I had to go around Hazel Avenue and come up Cobbs Creek and insist that I be allowed to go to 6221 [the MOVE house] so that maybe I could do something that would bring about a peaceful solution. . . . So I rang the bell, and Patricia Brooks Africa came to the door. I will never forget her face.

She began to talk about what brought them to the point where they were at that time. That was, their brothers and sisters were in jail. No one would listen to them, and the only way that they felt they could get an audience, to get anyone to listen, after exhausting all other measures through the legal means was to get on the loudspeaker. . . . And she told me that if they cursed, they knew they would bring attention because people would stop and listen. . . . I asked her what I could do. Could I help her. She said, go out and get the black press. . . .

It was too late to get any press people near the MOVE house.

CHAUNCEY CAMPBELL

Chauncey Campbell was another person who attempted to intervene. He was well known for his involvement in civil rights groups and in the Delaware Valley Citizen Concern Organization. He was also a member of the Executive Board of the West Philadelphia branch of the NAACP. On Mothers Day, May 12, 1985, some of his civil rights contacts asked him to talk to MOVE.

The police allowed him to approach the house. He met Patricia Brooks Africa with "two younger girls." He gave her his name. She went back in for a few minutes and then returned saying, "Oh, yeah, I understand you are a fair person."

He expressed his alarm that the police were sending in reinforcements and that the situation was becoming very dangerous. Campbell felt that Patricia Brooks understood and knew the danger. She asked him to go get permission for black reporters, community leaders, and ministers to come within range of the house so they could see that under no circumstances would MOVE initiate violence. She mentioned that their organization did not even believe in killing a fly.

According to Campbell, Patricia Africa felt MOVE had a constitutional right to express its outrage and that this was its way of expressing its rights. He recalled:

She was very impressive in her arguments. They wanted to express their outrage that their family members were imprisoned for killing the policemen, which they did not do. They felt this should be addressed. All they wanted from this confrontation was for someone to say that the issue would be addressed. They wanted commitments.

Patricia also mentioned that Jerry Africa was away from the house trying to negotiate, but they had lost contact with him and were worried. Campbell tried to find Jerry, feeling he was the key to untangling the situation. However, by the time he located Jerry, the police were not allowing anyone back in.

JUDGE ROBERT WILLIAMS

While Campbell was trying to locate Jerry Africa that Sunday, Jerry said he was at home waiting for a telephone call from Judge Robert Williams, Democratic candidate for district attorney.*

Jerry recalled, "They were expecting us not to negotiate. All we wanted to do was negotiate. Judge Williams sent his man out to the house on Osage Street. I don't remember his name, but he was involved in bringing Dick Gregory to our house in 1977 to negotiate."

Jerry indicated he and Judge Williams arranged a meeting for Saturday. It fell through. On Sunday they met at Williams's house. Jerry felt that Judge Williams expressed interest in resolving the matter peacefully. Apparently Jerry presented his legal argument about the invalidity of the convictions. The discussion with Judge Williams seems to have led to a variety of suggestions. One was for Judge Williams to try to get members of the Bar Association—"a lawyer we felt comfortable with and some that he [Judge Williams] felt comfortable with, to review all of this." They would then advise whether MOVE's rights had been violated.

He asked whether we would accept the Bar Association lawyers' opinion. I told him, "Certainly, because we know we are right." His ques-

*Since Judge Williams refused to be interviewed, this account is based entirely on the interview with Jerry Africa.

tion was, "Suppose you are wrong?" I said, "Then, we have a legal option to challenge his decision if he tried to manipulate the law and say that what happened did not happen that way."

This idea went no further.

Another approach Judge Williams and Jerry Africa discussed was for Williams to contact Chief Justice Nix of the Pennsylvania Supreme Court to review the legal points. Appeals were mired in midlevel review court procedures and had not been presented to the Pennsylvania Supreme Court. Jerry assured him that if Nix reviewed it and granted bail, to be followed by a more in-depth review, MOVE would cease the confrontation.

They could not get in touch with Justice Nix. They tried to call Mayor Goode but were told he was out of town. Jerry told Judge Williams he had to get back home, his family [MOVE] would be trying to call him. He would wait by the telephone in case Judge Williams contacted Goode or Nix. He never heard from Judge Williams again.

OTHER LAST-MINUTE ATTEMPTS

Bennie Swans from the CIN and Bob Owens also made a last-minute attempt. Swans said that on the night of May 12, with the approval of the police commissioner and the city managing director, he made one last attempt to head off the confrontation planned for the next morning. Swans and Bob Owens, a childhood friend of Conrad Africa, went to the MOVE house around nine in the evening. Swans testified to the MOVE commission:

We engaged in discussion with Conrad in terms of the issue of the children . . . is there another vehicle which they could use to raise their point of concern regarding the release of the persons that were arrested in '78? We looked at options. There was no hostility. There was complete control of his [Conrad's] faculties and there was a decision that the confrontation in his view was inevitable and that he appreciated the dialogue. However, they were not going to leave the compound unless there was, in fact, the release of those persons. . . .[6]

Swans asked Conrad to allow the children to be released from the house. He said Conrad replied, "MOVE children are not going to anyone else's house. They are in their house. Our children are with us, and we plan for them to stay with us." Swans's testimony to the MOVE Commission continued thus:

Q. At the end of this conversation, did you, sir, feel that there were any additional possibilities of avoiding the confrontation through continued negotiation or discussion with Conrad?

A. I believe that there is always a chance as long as the lines of communications remain open . . .

Q. Did that end your conversation with Conrad Africa?

A. That ended the discussion. Bob Owens, who again is extremely close with Conrad, they clasped. Bob had really gotten pretty upset, he had tears in his eyes. Conrad appeared to me to be extremely sensitive to the issue that he was being confronted with. And after they clasped hands, he went back to Osage Avenue and Conrad went back into the MOVE compound. . . . [7]

Chauncey Campbell mentioned two other last-minute attempts. One was by Alfonso Deal, the president of the largest NAACP branch in Pennsylvania. He had been involved as a policeman in the 1978 MOVE situation and received "a lot of static for making a statement pertaining to MOVE's rights." He eventually retired from the police department and was elected to the state legislature. Deal knew people in the MOVE house personally. Campbell mused, "Being a state legislator with the NAACP you'd expect that he would have no problem going there and negotiating. He asked for permission to go in the building, and he was not allowed."

After the assault began and there was a lull in the shooting, Campbell heard the mayor say over television that they were attempting negotiations.

I got all excited on hearing that. I was rushing back to tell Louise James, owner of the Osage Avenue MOVE house, the good news that everything was going to be all right. Then I heard a boom.

You would never believe what negotiation Goode was talking about. The negotiation was a few people, maybe three or four or better coming down to the house, maybe within about two football fields' distance, and with a loudspeaker saying, "Come out." Whether MOVE could hear that, especially if they were in the back of the building, there is no way they could hear anything. But that is supposed to be the negotiation.

Campbell may have been referring to the Committee of Humanity and Dignity. According to Stanley Vaughn:

We had formed a committee which was called the Committee of Humanity and Dignity, right there on the scene [on Osage on May 13], which consisted of the clergy and some community persons and a couple of leaders in the area. We got together, and we were completely opposed to what was going on—the hoses and all of the police around the house. So we went to the mayor. The mayor had allowed us to go and negotiate. We were given bullhorns. In a situation like that everybody using a bullhorn sounds like the police, especially when you are in a situation like the MOVE people were.[8]

Nothing resulted from the attempt.

WHY THERE WAS NO EFFECTIVE THIRD-PARTY INTERVENTION

Various factors contributed to the lack of an extended and systematic effort to prevent the May 13, 1985 confrontation between MOVE and the city of Philadelphia.

The Political Environment

The political environment in Philadelphia in 1985 was vastly different from the pre-1978 period. The city had moved from the confrontational, racially polarized Rizzo era to the Greene administration, which provided a healing period. By 1985 Wilson Goode was in charge as the first black mayor. He had strong liberal backing. It was inconceivable to many that this administration would engage in violently repressive tactics. MOVE by now was almost entirely black, the city administration was controlled by a black mayor, and the neighborhood was black. No one thought of needing to organize a pressure group to ensure that the city acted fairly. Anyone who tried would have had to organize in a community that was the heart of Goode's political support.

Unlike Powelton, which was a stronghold of political opposition, Osage residents backed the mayor. They trusted him not to engage in tactics that could harm the community. Thus, there was no pressure for organizing as there had been in 1978, when CCCHR was able to mobilize broad public support for a negotiated settlement.

City Administrators' Perceptions

Except for District Attorney Ed Rendell, no one in a leadership position had been directly involved in the 1978 conflict. They apparently relied on the folk history of that confrontation. Those in power, and the public at large, seem to have reached the conclusion that it was impossible to negotiate with MOVE. Newspaper reports that MOVE "broke" the 1978 agreement, coupled with the recollections of some of the intervenors of that period, left the impression that MOVE was an unreliable negotiator. They felt that MOVE either was too crazy to carry out an agreement or did not see it as politically advantageous to do so. For example, Lary Groth, deputy director of the Commission on Human Relations, pointed out that after working with MOVE over the years, he had an understanding of how they operated. He said, "Human Relations failed because Clarence Farmer and Lary Groth could not convince people that . . . no one could negotiate with MOVE."

Even though the evidence indicates that MOVE was constantly trying to open lines of communication to negotiate, many people felt MOVE's strategy was confrontational. The public saw it as not wanting to negotiate and pressing nonnegotiable demands.

Groth, Farmer, and Washington expressed the prevailing view that the issue "freedom for the political prisoners" was an unreasonable demand that only underlined MOVE's irrationality. On the other hand, Oscar Gaskins, the attorney who broke through a similar conceptual problem with the release of the three prisoners in 1978, did not see it as a nonnegotiable or dead-end issue. However, he pointed out that in 1985 no one asked him to be involved as an intermediary.

Gaskins said:

I don't pretend to be much of a negotiator [but the situation in 1985 was just like in 1978]. Everybody else stood back then and said, "Well, we have prisoners in jail. . . . We can't get them out of jail because they are murderers." Once you take that approach, and say you can't do anything, that shuts off negotiations. That would never be my approach.

Fact of the matter is, they were convicted of third-degree murder. In the traditional sense, there is a question as to whether or not they are murderers as we understand murderers to be—certainly not all of them. The thing that is amazing is they tried nine of them for murdering Officer Ramp. There are some real questions where the bullet . . . came from. Those women could not have all been guilty. There were not enough guns in the basement for everybody to have a gun, so they convicted them on a conspiracy charge and then uniformly gave them 30- to 100-year sentences.

First of all, MOVE people are reasonably bright and would know what the city can do and what the city cannot do. Second, there is a serious question as to whether they ever hoped to get the murderers out. But you have some people in jail like Jerry Africa's girlfriend [Alberta Wicker Africa], who has been in jail since 1978. She was only charged with standing up on the platform and inciting to riot. She has been in jail now for seven years. You can charge some of that to the fact that she's been a bad prisoner, but her minimum sentence has expired. So there is no reason why she should be there. Any reasonable-thinking person would have found a way to get her out in light of a major confrontation. As a matter of fact, at the end of this long . . . time, there is no reason why they could not have gotten some of the other people out.

The perception that MOVE's demand was nonnegotiable might have been the major reason for the city's decision to treat the MOVE problem as a police matter and to discourage civilian involvement in resolving the conflict.

Police Perceptions

Another factor might have been police perceptions of the effect of third-party intervention on the 1978 crisis. They may have felt that the long period of negotiations only focused more public attention on the confrontation. That attention limited the options available to the police, setting up the situation in which a policeman was killed. It seems that a primary concern of the police in 1985 was to avoid injury to the officers at any cost. One observer wrote:

Arguably . . . history [the 1978 shootout] made the police on Osage Avenue unduly wary of personal risk, thus tending towards a no-muss-no-fuss solution like the dropping of a bomb. In brief conversations I had with police officers, there was a sense that this operation [the May 13 assault] had been successful. "We didn't make the mistake we made last time," said one officer at the barricade on Pine Street. "The lesson of '78 was that the strategy should be controlled and careful," said Frank Selgrath, an editor of the Police Union newspaper, *Peace Officer*. "Though it seems ludicrous to say so, every action was taken to see that there was no loss of life or property." . . . Although the police should be pleased that they lost no one this time, the other bottom line is this: in 1978, 11 children were rescued from the MOVE house, in 1985, only one child was saved while four burned to death.[9]

David Fattah, of the House of Umoja, argued that nothing had been done over the years to resolve the hostility between the police rank and file and MOVE. The tension was similar to two gangs that had engaged in a fight, and one lost. He recalled seeing graffiti in a police precinct that read "MOVE 1, Police 0," implying a desire to even the score. This view seems to be substantiated by Mayor Goode's order to the police commissioner that officers who were directly involved in the 1978 shoot-out should not be involved in the Osage assault.*[10] This need to "even the score" would encourage police to take charge of the situation themselves, and to avoid citizen intervention.

Bennie Swans pointed out an ironic twist. It was the Civil Affairs Division of the Philadelphia Police Department that asked him to be involved in the 1985 Osage Avenue crisis. It is puzzling that he was prevented from following through on the request because higher city officials had defined the problem as

---

*The police commissioner contradicted the mayor's testimony that such an order had been given.

one for the police to handle. He speculated that someone in the Civil Affairs Division must have acted without authorization when he was asked to be involved.

The Role of Neighbors

Some have described Mayor Goode's policy as "wait and see" or "do nothing." Trying to wait out a conflict in the hope that it will dissipate is a commonly used form of conflict management. In this case, however, the mayor's decision to ignore the problem only succeeded in alienating the Osage neighbors. It boxed him into a situation where his only option was to take drastic action. The city's nonresponse made some neighbors threaten to take the law in their own hands, or in other instances to go over the mayor and appeal directly to the governor for help. It became such a media event that the mayor was pressured to do something quickly and dramatically to restore confidence. Hence, failure to take timely action might have created constraints that precluded negotiation, which needs time and patience.

Limitations of City-Sponsored Crisis Units

Another problem may have been the limitations of city-sponsored crisis units. It is ironic that when the mayor was the managing director, he developed the City Intervention Program precisely to defuse community and racial tensions and avoid crises such as the Osage situation. However, this agency was never used or consulted when making the decision to confront MOVE. The agencies and personnel that were coordinated by the City Intervention Program had a solid reservoir of expertise in peaceful conflict resolution but were unable to act.

Without express authorization, two of the agencies under the City Intervention Program, the Philadelphia Human Relations Commission and the CIN, tried to play some role in 1985. Apparently neither felt it could be actively involved in mediating this conflict when the city, as one party to the conflict, had decided not to negotiate.

When Farmer left his directorship of the Human Relations

Commission in March 1985, his open-door policy went with him. Jerry Africa had seen Farmer as a person who was always available, who would use his influence for MOVE. Absent that contact, the last communications channel with the city was gone. Jerry Africa remarked that the only avenue left was the bullhorn.

Bennie Swans' intervention plan might have put MOVE and the Osage neighbors on common ground. However, even if he had not been explicitly instructed by the city to stay out, it is doubtful that he would have had the freedom to use his approach. His strategy would have forged an alliance between MOVE and the neighborhood to pressure the city for a settlement. This approach might have worked, but it was not likely to give a city-funded agency a sense of financial security.

Few cities sponsor as many conflict-resolution agencies as Philadelphia. However, the agencies' dependence on city funding hamstrung them when it came to a sensitive conflict in which the city was a party.

Lack of Independent Outside Mediators

In addition to the limitations of city-funded agencies, the lack of independent third-parties that had long-term relationships with the conflict parties was a major shortcoming in 1985. People who had served as intermediaries in the past were reluctant to become involved again. They remembered the months of thankless labor and fatigue they spent mediating the 1978 problem. Involvement meant a tremendous sacrifice of time and energy. For example, Walter Palmer commented, "You would have to pay me to do the same intervention work this time. It was too exhausting." Those non-city funded intermediaries that became involved in 1985 did not have a long-term relationship with MOVE and the city and were unable to establish trust with the parties. One MOVE member complained about the mediators:

The persecution of MOVE was going on long before May 1985. . . . Nobody was getting involved. The situation existed for them to get involved. When you look at that, you got to ask—what do you think of a person who gets involved and jumps on the bandwagon after it gets rolling? They aren't doing it from the heart. They are doing it for the credit, notoriety and publicity. That is why you see them here one day and gone tomorrow.

In contrast, Jerry Africa presented a positive view of Clarence Farmer: "He played a key role. If other people had used their influence the way he attempted to use his, we probably would not have had a May 13, 1985." The difference with Farmer was that he had established an open-door early in the conflict. He maintained a relationship with MOVE at the beginning and kept communication open as long as he was in office. James Laue argues:

Good crisis intervention consumes much interpersonal capital. That capital should be built between the third party and the other parties in non-crisis situations. Rather than first meeting the parties when they are arrayed for battle, an intervenor would rather have relationships already built through a long period of specific, targeted, focused intervention.[11]

In short, for an intermediary to be successful, he or she need not only be structurally and financially independent of the parties but also should develop the "interpersonal capital" in order to be taken seriously by the parties when intervention occurs.

POST 1985

Had the MOVE/Philadelphia conflict burned itself out in the rubble at Osage Avenue? By 1986 there were indications that the dispute still smoldered. According to most sources, Vincent Leophart, MOVE's founder, perished in the May 13 fire. However, all the MOVE members interviewed maintained that John Africa still lives. Ramona Africa, the only adult member known to have escaped the fire, was sentenced to prison for 16 months to 7 years on charges of riot and conspiracy stemming from the conflagration.

MOVE continued to maintain a presence in Philadelphia, although soon after the bombing Philadelphia newspapers reported there were fewer than half a dozen active members who were not in prison. However, MOVE members or followers owned or rented eight properties in Philadelphia. In late 1986, 5 MOVE women and possibly 15 children lived at 1630 S. 56th St. in Southwest Philadelphia. Once again, they began to board up their quarters and reinforce it.[12]

MOVE members also claimed that they were broadening their support and recruiting converts in the prisons. Seven imprisoned members who had played leadership roles in the past would be eligible for parole before 1990.[13]

Newspapers speculated that the old MOVE leadership had been decimated, and the new structure was unclear. Many saw Jerry Africa as a possible future leader. When interviewed late in 1986, Jerry Africa maintained that he was still talking to anyone who would listen. He continued to press his claim for "justice" for MOVE's prisoners. The bombing did not change the issue. It may have expanded it, though. Louise James, who owned the Osage MOVE house and was John Africa's sister, maintained in her testimony to the MOVE Commission, "Everyone connected with the killing of my family [must go] to jail."

While Philadelphians hoped for a return to normalcy, Jerry Africa warned:

There's not going to be any peace . . . as long as . . . there are innocent people in prison. What do you expect for us to do? It is not for us to correct. It is for them to correct. On numerous occasions they have tried to give the impression they want to resolve this thing without any more bloodshed or friction. We cooperated to the fullest, and they spit on our face again. We don't have to take this. We have been tolerant with the city, with its methods and approach, and they have yet to come up with any viable solutions to correct this.

What do we do? Tell me where we can go. We know what we are going to do. The point is, people have got to die; not because we want to die. This is the price they are making us pay in order to expose their crimes.

The imprisoned MOVE members perceived a continuation of the conflict and their "persecution" within the prison system. As an example, Delbert Africa cited the parole problems Ramona Africa faced. She was sentenced to a minimum of 16 months and a maximum of 7 years for riot and conspiracy charges arising from the May 13, 1985, bombing. Under Pennsylvania law prisoners could be granted parole after they have served half of their minimum term. Ramona Africa's first parole hearing was held December 22, 1986. She might have been granted parole if she had agreed to certain conditions. Among them were " . . . that you not associate with the MOVE organization in any way, including visiting the premises of MOVE households." The parole report also cited "strenuous objections of the District Attorney."[14]

Delbert Africa argued that this was persecution of the MOVE organization:

If you are Catholic and you get out of [prison], are they going to tell you not to go to church anymore? It's not done with anybody else. I know members of the Black Muslims that got so-called crimes connected with their religious affiliation, but they don't tell them don't go around the mosque no more. They don't tell them don't be around the Fruit of Islam no more. It is only done with MOVE.

Both Delbert and Phil Africa also pointed out another instance of what they called selective law enforcement and oppression. Since their conviction for the Powelton shoot-out in 1981, the MOVE prisoners were generally kept with the regular inmates until May 15, 1985, two days after the Osage bombing. Then they were moved to the Restrictive Housing Unit (RHU), known by prisoners as "the hole." The RHU is a place where dangerous prisoners and rule breakers are held in isolation from the general population. The inmates in the RHU receive fewer privileges than the regular prisoners and their cases are reviewed periodically.

Phil and Delbert understood that they were confined in the RHU initially because the prison authorities feared they might respond violently to the news that their family has been killed in the bombing. Phil stated:

After keepin' us in the hole for 17 days without a misconduct write-up, we were given write-ups on the 17th day for not cutting our hair, *clearly* an excuse to justify our being kept in the hole. We have been in this prison since August of 1981, had explained to the prison officials in 1981 the religious purpose of our hair and had been told by both deputy superintendents that there would be no harassment of us about our hair.[15]

Delbert and Phil Africa said they had been confined in the RHU nearly two years because of their hair. The prison administrators, however, pointed out that the reason was not their hair, but their disruptive behaviors, such as assaulting other prisoners, and inciting riots in the prison.

While prison administrators maintained that they followed routine procedure, MOVE prisoners argued, as they had in Philadelphia, that they were the victims of selective law enforcement. Phil forecast that their RHU confinement would evolve into another May 13 type of confrontation.

We'll have to write letters about it. We'll have to keep speaking about it. The more we speak out about it, the madder they will get at us. They will want to get us to shut up. We'll get the inmates in the general population to say, "They been in the hole for two years. That's wrong. Let's do something about it." This will get the prison authorities upset and they will jump on us. But we didn't do nothing wrong.

In short, one year after the bombing one could identify potential grounds for future conflicts both between MOVE and the city of Philadelphia and between MOVE and the prison system.

NOTES

1. Transcript of the Philadelphia Special Commission to Investigate the MOVE Crisis, *Philadelphia Inquirer,* Oct. 28, 1985, special section, p. 4-C.
2. Ibid.
3. Ibid.
4. Ibid.
5. "The Bombing of West Philly," *Frontline,* Public Television Service Documentary, May 6, 1987, transcribed by the authors.
6. Transcript, p. 4-C.
7. Ibid.

8. "Bombing on Osage Avenue," WHYY TV, 1987, documentary. Transcribed by the authors.

9. Phillip Weiss, "How He Bombed in Philadelphia: Goode, Bad, and Ugly," *The New Republic,* June 10, 1985, p. 12.

10. Transcript, p. 9-C.

11. James H. Laue, "Third Party Roles in Community Conflict: The MOVE Experience," *Conflict Resolution Notes* 4, no. 2 (Sept. 1986): p. 14.

12. Kitty Caparella, "Will MOVE Rise Again?" *Philadelphia Daily News,* Mar. 24, 1986, p. 19.

13. Ibid.

14. Commonwealth of Pennsylvania, Board of Probation and Parole, Notice of Board Decision, re. Ramona Johnson Africa, Dec. 22, 1986.

15. Phillip Africa, MOVE document, dated Jan. 21, 1987. (Photocopy.)

9

Conclusions

Key questions remain after having sifted through the two tragic confrontations between MOVE and the city of Philadelphia: Could the conflict with MOVE be resolved peacefully? What insights could be drawn from this experience that would apply to resolving other similar conflicts?

MOVE AND CONFLICT RESOLUTION

Is it possible to resolve the conflicts with MOVE peacefully? Or is violence the only alternative to deal with this conflict? To a certain extent, the answer to this question depends on one's assessment of MOVE's basic nature, the motivation of the members, and whether one perceives MOVE as able to comprehend and respect negotiated processes.

Frederick Hacker has developed three classifications to describe groups that engage in violent confrontation with governments and organized society: crazies, criminals, and crusaders.[1] If MOVE members are crazy, i.e., insane, or of unsound mind, then rational and peaceful processes such as negotiation and mediation would not work. The members would lack the capacity to control their behaviors and could not enter into an agreement to regulate their actions in the future. On the other hand, if MOVE is a group of "criminals" or "crusaders," there might be some underlying rationality to their thinking that would indicate negotiated settlement is possible. The question of whether negotiation with these groups is effective or desirable will be addressed later.

According to Hacker:

[C]riminal[s] . . . want nothing different from what most other people want, but they are willing to resort to socially disapproved methods in order to achieve their goals. Crusaders [on the other hand] . . . are ideally inspired. They seek, not personal gain, but prestige and power for a collective goal; they believe that they act in the service of a higher cause.[2]

To find out which of Hacker's three categories might appropriately describe MOVE, we went back to the question that we raised at the beginning of this book and posed it to the many people who interacted with MOVE. We asked several intervenors and neighbors what they thought MOVE was.

Ann Doley of Powelton Village, who was actively involved in neighborhood organizing and legal activities to stop the police blockade against MOVE, answered:

Everybody views MOVE as fairly crazy. We had an accurate view. We had day-to-day dealings with them. I see them as a cult very similar to Jonestown. They were "true believers." They weren't all the lumpen poor. Some were creative, talented, brilliant, amazingly sensitive people. They just had some vulnerability from what has happened in society. This filled some need in their lives.

I don't think they are dangerous. Only to the level that if you became the object of a lot of their hate, you could get into a fistfight with them. You could also choose to stay away.

They developed a siege mentality. Their view of reality is just so different than ours. By living in the house for a year under siege, all the craziness became compounded and became the ordinary way of living for them. They came to love confrontation.

Another Powelton resident, Dave Kairys, a PUN lawyer who filed a petition with the Pennsylvania Supreme Court to stop the 1978 blockade against MOVE, stated:

Whenever Rizzo was in political trouble, he had to concoct a scheme which consistently involves threats to white people by black people.

Once it was an attempt to assassinate him, at another time it was supposedly an attempt to blow up large portions of the city. In the 1978 confrontation, Rizzo, unlike his usual tactics with black political groups, sat on the situation for over a year, playing it up to the media at any chance he had. MOVE fit the stereotype that whites tend to fear most in black people. . . . It seemed clear to me at the time, and has seemed so since to me and many others, that the MOVE situation was dragged out unnecessarily and primed for the media to wind up in a confrontation just when Rizzo needed one. Besides its obvious importance to the whole history, I believe this tactic by Rizzo had the effect of creating a siege mentality that became a basic component of MOVE's thinking. It is no surprise to me that as soon as they moved to a new house, for instance, they began barricading it and preparing for a siege.

Sister Falaka Fattah, director of the House of Umoja, a Muslim religious and community leader, was involved in providing support for MOVE during the 1977 blockade and knew the members long before this event. She described MOVE thus: "They were like missionaries. My first impression was that it was a religion, and I think I took that position basically because I studied comparative religion. If you look at the beginnings of many religions, the practices are very weird."

Bennie Swans, director of the CIN, who tried to involve federal and state intermediaries in the problem, saw MOVE as a revolutionary organization:

MOVE had grown out of the revolutionary period of blacks in this country. It talked about a different value system. It was concerned about caging of animals and the desire to free themselves both in the mind and spirit from the system. Group living became a vehicle. [In the mid 1970s] it began to deal with those kinds of issues that impacted negatively on neighborhoods.

Oscar Gaskins, the attorney who represented MOVE in its negotiations with the city in 1978, recalled, "You weren't dealing with fringe people. We were dealing with pretty intelligent people. Delbert was a college student. Someone else had graduated from Penn State."

Walter Palmer, an organizer of the Citywide Community Coalition for Human Rights in 1978, answered:

MOVE was rooted in the black street, as opposed to middle class, existence. Basically they were a small faction of people who were involved in confrontation on society's abuses in general and police abuse in specific. Not everybody could talk with MOVE, but I could because I come from the same kind of background.

Joel Todd, an attorney for Jerry Africa who later attempted to mediate the MOVE-city dispute said:

It is a messianic revolutionary organization. The members are not crazy. They are committed, fully committed, to their goals of doing away with technology. They are ready to die for their beliefs. They go about provoking confrontation because they are revolutionary. They have absolutely no interest in peaceful coexistence. Some are college-educated and very likable people.

Lary Groth, deputy director of the Philadelphia Commission on Human Relations, saw MOVE thus: "They weren't mentally unbalanced. It was never unconscious irrationality. It was conscious irrationality. They knew what they were doing from the very beginning. They pushed the city all over the place; in both cases always with the understanding that they could get what they wanted.

Throughout most of the 1977-78 period, intermediaries met with Robert, Delbert, and either Conrad or Phil Africa. Even though John Africa was MOVE's founder and coordinator he was apparently always in the background. Few intervenors saw him as playing a major role in the actual negotiations. Robert Africa was described as college-educated, articulate, and a thinker. While Farmer described Delbert as highly confrontational and crazy, other intervenors who worked with him found he could negotiate. Farmer thought part of the problem was that the more moderate Robert lost control to the more confrontational leadership surrounding Delbert. Msgr. Charles Devlin, who negotiated with Delbert, saw the confrontation taking place because Delbert lost influence to others who were more confrontational.

From the above interviews, a consensus seems to emerge that portrays MOVE members as "crusaders" rather than insane or mentally unbalanced "crazies." One could therefore expect that MOVE members would be able to understand and engage in rational processes such as dialogue and problem solving.

However, even if in the abstract one could argue that dialogue and problem solving approaches such as negotiation and mediation could possibly work with MOVE, a question still remains whether it would be possible to negotiate the differences between MOVE and the city, especially given MOVE's extremist rhetoric. Often, mediation and negotiation are viewed as processes where give and take occur and the parties are willing to accommodate each other's needs. Each side gives a little until an agreement is reached that both parties can work with. However, in this conflict, MOVE's position sounded uncompromising:

> We refuse to compromise our belief because we know and can prove our belief is right. John Africa equips us with the understanding that when you compromise what is right, you are no longer right, you no longer have what is right, you have something other than right which can only be wrong. John Africa wisely explains that you cannot add to or subtract from what is right and still have what is right.[3]

Joel Todd, on the other hand, described MOVE's values by saying, "The basic truth is that what these people believed in was a total anathema to an organized society."

There seems to be a basic value conflict here that gives the situation a zero-sum appearance; that is, one party has to lose in order for the other to gain. Does it mean, however, that negotiation and mediation are not viable where there is basic value conflict between the parties? An experienced mediator, Laura Blackburne points out, "When you have differing values and differing perspectives, it simply makes conflict resolution more difficult, it does not make it impossible."[4] It can be argued that even in cases of major value conflict, negotiation, assisted by third-party intermediaries, would still be possible, although the role of the third party as interpreter and creative problem solver would be crucial. In this kind of conflict, the third party could aim for at least one of three alternative objectives:

The first, and probably the most preferred, would be for the intervenor to encourage the parties to redefine both their problems and the values that pertain to the problems. Often the labels and the language parties use to present their initial positions obscure the true nature of their mutual problems and make discussions difficult. It is possible that once the parties go beyond the hurdle of labeling their beliefs and positions and start to jointly define the true nature of their needs, they may find some common ground on which a solution could be built.

If this objective is not attainable, a second alternative could be to help the parties discover a creative solution that does not sacrifice each party's basic values and world view. The composting agreement between MOVE and the Powelton neighbors provides a good example. Delbert Africa stated:

As long as whatever has been asked of us didn't violate our beliefs, we would find a way to accommodate what we saw as the resistance in the person's mind. [Concerning the odor generated by MOVE's recycling of food scraps] I tried to explain [to the neighbors] that the odor isn't killing you. I can understand that you are not used to it. But if the person was just intent, stuck in a rut, couldn't accept it, I would try to work it out. We could turn in the earth and get some exercise doing it.

This approach produced compost, which was useful in some of the neighbors' gardens. Delbert Africa observed, "We had people throughout the neighborhood we would sell the compost to."

The composting agreement represented a case where the parties were able to create an alternative proposal that expanded the range of the solutions without sacrificing any of their fundamental beliefs. MOVE was able to act according to its belief in recycling its refuse. In addition, it ended up with another exercise regime and a small source of income. The neighbors maintained their value of keeping their neighborhood clean by reducing the odor level and at the same time got a source of fertilizer for their gardens.

Another example of such a creative approach was Gaskins'

proposal to break the deadlock over MOVE's 1976 demand for the release of their already convicted and sentenced leaders. On the surface, demanding their release seemed to directly contradict mainstream society's values and belief in an orderly judicial process. But Gaskins was able to address the release issue without compromising the city's value of the dignity of the law, and MOVE'S need for freedom for its imprisoned members. He enabled both parties to come to an acceptable settlement without giving up their basic values.

Even in the 1985 deadlock over MOVE's demand for the release of the ten convicted prisoners, Gaskins offered a suggestion that could have expanded the range of solutions. It could have been accepted by both contenders in the conflict without feeling that they had sacrificed their fundamental beliefs.

If either of these two objectives of the intervenor is not attainable because the parties' value differences are too great to allow for conflict resolution, a third alternative objective for the intermediary could be conflict containment and management. The basic question for the intermediary is: Even if the long-run objectives of the two parties are mutually incompatible, what can be done in the short run to make peaceful coexistence possible? This approach emphasizes avoiding crisis and monitoring day-to-day interactions. It seeks to defuse small conflicts early enough to prevent them from becoming glamorized and linked to larger principles and value systems. This objective requires that intervention attempts be made at the lowest level possible. Trained and qualified mediators would have to be available in the community to intervene quickly.* This process could educate the parties that it is possible to interact with each other on some basic levels even though they disagree on ultimate objectives. It could build trust by reducing each party's fears about the other's intentions, and this trust could be the threshold for long-range conflict resolution. The principle of détente between the Eastern and Western bloc countries, supposedly two incompatible ideological blocs, is based on these premises.

*For a detailed discussion of the characteristics, skills, and qualifications required of a successful mediator, see Hizkias Assefa, *Mediation of Civil Wars: Approaches and Strategies*, Boulder, CO: Westview Press, 1987, Chs. 2, 8.

Therefore, mediation and negotiation could play important roles even in conflicts that involve apparent value incompatibilities or positions that are stated in extreme terms. Even if the conflict might not be resolved, it could be managed or contained so that violent confrontations such as those of August 8, 1978, or May 13, 1985, are avoided.

So far the conflict resolution mechanisms discussed have been negotiation and mediation. How about the other third-party dispute-resolution mechanisms, such as adjudication and arbitration? Are they equally viable?

The latter two processes are based on a search for right and wrong, using some prescribed criteria. Adjudication can work where both parties accept the rules of the game and recognize the legitimacy and authority of the judicial body. MOVE members, however, did not. To them the court and its alien laws were only an arm of the "system" that they were fighting against. They could only perceive court rulings as one more way for the "system" to impose its will. Hence, adjudication only escalated the conflict, and that is why it demonstrably failed to avoid the tragic confrontations of 1978 and 1985.

Christopher Mitchell argues:

Increasingly in Western industrial societies we are beginning to see conflicts that are "international" (Type I) in the way some people regard them, even though they take place within a framework of politics and rule which we normally regard as "national" (Type II). International conflicts are conflicts between two parties that regard themselves as equally sovereign. If you have a conflict which at least one side defines at a Type I conflict, that is, a conflict between equally sovereign parties with equally legitimate claims, then to treat it within a Type II management framework [like the courts] just will not work.[5]

Court systems assume both parties acknowledge the supremacy of the state and the legal system.

Arbitration, where the parties first agree on a third party who then renders judgment, avoids the problem of the decision maker appearing to be an arm of one party. The suggestion during the Osage Avenue conflict to set up a panel that would establish some procedure to review the 1981 MOVE convictions approximated an arbitration procedure. It is unlikely, however, that arbitration would have worked in the MOVE dispute. The arbitrator most likely would have to render a decision in which one party would win and the other would lose, using legal criteria that MOVE does not recognize. Thus, the most viable mechanisms for handling Type I conflicts are negotiation and mediation.

GENERAL LESSONS

Are there general lessons to be drawn from the MOVE experience concerning peaceful resolution of similar conflicts? In many ways, the issues involved in the MOVE conflict were unique. However, the tactics used by MOVE in its confrontation with the city have been characterized by the press as similar to those used by many other fringe groups in contemporary society, such as hostage takers and terrorists. It has been pointed out that MOVE held the Osage neighborhood hostge by harassing the neighbors until the city addressed MOVE's demands. Even though MOVE members pointed out that they never initiated violence, they raised the specter of terror by displaying weapons and by claiming to have wired the neighborhood with bombs. Finally, in effect, they held their own children as hostages by refusing to allow them to be removed from the scene of the conflict when police attack became imminent. One wonders, therefore, if the MOVE-Philadelphia conflict might provide some insight into the peaceful resolution of conflicts involving extremist fringe groups and hostage takers.

Many argue that there is little role for nonviolent conflict resolution in these cases. They suggest that one should not negotiate with hostage takers, since this might encourage repetition of their conduct. The best approach, it is argued, is to communicate toughness and resolve by refusing to deal with hostage takers and take counterterrorist measures if they do not surrender. This approach generally relegates the handling of the conflict to law enforcement or military personnel.

It is far from clear that this tough policy works. Where the hostage takers are "crusaders" who are prepared to kill themselves for their cause, it might only raise the stakes and challenge them to hit even more vulnerable spots. MOVE's hardened position after the 1985 shoot-out illustrates this point: "This system thinks that . . . dropping the bomb on our house . . . murdering our family will stop the MOVE organization. . . . But nothing this system does will stop . . . the MOVE organization. Anything they do to us only makes us come back at them that much harder and stronger."

Thus, reliance on force to the exclusion of negotiation might only create a false sense of security. Moreover, the MOVE-Philadelphia confrontation illustrates another problem with the violent approach. It may temporarily terminate the conflict but seldom will resolve it. If the conflict is deep, a forced settlement that does not address the root causes of the dispute only sows the seeds of future conflicts. The 1978 MOVE shoot-out set the stage for 1985, and the potential for another conflict remained after the 1985 bombing.

Negotiation and mediation allow the parties to explore and treat the root causes of the conflict. To reach that point, the parties need to understand that they do not show weakness by undertaking nonviolent approaches. There is room to negotiate with hostage takers short of unilateral capitulation to their demands. Miller argues: "Terrorism is after all the political weapon of the weak. . . . A weak opponent is also an opponent who needs a victory, even if it is only face saving and symbolic. This means, . . . that there is much latitude for governments to pursue in the context of the bargaining process."[6]

Organizations or individuals who undertake to mediate or negotiate in a terrorist situation must be prepared for the negative outcry that may arise. They are liable to be attacked on moral grounds that they are according terrorists the prestige of being treated as equal negotiators; they are rewarding violent behavior; and it is immoral to enforce an agreement concluded under threat.[7] However, Hacker argues that if this were true, then society is already guilty of encouraging terrorism because authorities do bargain with blackmailers, kidnappers, and even terrorists where the stakes are high. Prosecutors negotiate with murderers under the name of plea bargaining.[8]

When negotiations or other peaceful approaches are pitted against the use of force in hostage taking or terrorist conflicts,

violence has an instinctual appeal. It promises instant and spec-
tacular solutions. In contrast, the nonviolent approaches of negotiation and mediation appear to be too soft or to indicate
weakness. They provide few opportunities for the participants
to visibly demonstrate socially cherished characteristics of cour-
age and heroism. They require time, patience, an ability to cope
with complexity, flexibility, imagination, skepticism of precon-
ceived biases and prescriptions.

Nonviolent intervention aims at long-term relationships and
often requires restructuring patterns of thinking and feeling.
Despite the complexity of their job, peaceful conflict resolvers
receive little praise. If intervention is successful, the parties take
credit. When this happens, it is easy for an intervenor's feelings
to be bruised, such as when Sister Falakah Fattah complained
that John Africa took credit for all the efforts that brought about
the May 5, 1978 agreement between MOVE and the city. On
the other hand, the intervenor is the convenient one to blame
when negotiations fail. Intervenors must have the strength of
character to carry on in their search for long-lasting solutions.
The challenge to the potential nonviolent conflict resolver is
that the ego rewards are scarce, but the potential for effective
peacemaking is high.

NOTES

1. Frederick Hacker, *Crusaders, Criminals, Crazies. Terror and Terrorism
in Our Time* (New York: W. W. Norton, 1976), p. 8.
2. Ibid.
3. MOVE document, undated.
4. Laura Blackburne, transcript of remarks at "Community Conflict
Resolution: Lessons from the MOVE Experience," conference cospon-
sored by the Fellowship Commission and the Conflict Resolution Center, Inc., Philadelphia, May 12, 1986, p. 1.
5. Christopher Mitchell, "Six Puzzles About Community Conflicts: The
MOVE Situation," *Conflict Resolution Notes* 4, 2 (Sept. 1986): 15.
6. Abraham Miller, *Terrorism and Hostage Negotiations* (Boulder, CO:
Westview Press, 1980), pp. 25-26.
7. Hacker, *Crusaders . . .* p. 265.
8. Ibid.

Bibliography

GENERAL

Assefa, Hizkias, *Mediation of Civil Wars: Approaches and Strategies—The Sudan Conflict,* Boulder, CO: Westview Press, 1987.

Asuncion-Lande, Nobleza, and Deanna Womack, "Communication and Conflict Management Across Cultures." Paper presented at the International Political Science Association, Twelfth International Congress, Rio de Janeiro, August 9-14, 1982.

Barnett, Robin, Bay Manning, Roger Meyer, and Georgia Quinones. *A Manual for Resolving Large Group Conflicts.* San Francisco: Community Board Program, 1986.

Carpenter, Susan L. "Managing Environmental Disputes." *Peace and Change* 3, no. 1 (Summer 1982) pp. 105-115.

Curle, Adam. *In the Middle: Non-Official Mediation in Violent Situations.* New York: St. Martin's Press, 1986.

Fisher, Roger, and William Ury. *Getting to Yes: Negotiating Agreement Without Giving In.* Boston: Houghton Mifflin, 1981.

Hacker, Frederick. *Crusaders, Criminals, Crazies. Terror and Terrorism in Our Time.* New York: W. W. Norton, 1976.

Kochman, Thomas. *Black and White Styles in Conflict.* Chicago: University of Chicago Press, 1981.

———. "The Politics of Politeness: Social Warrants in Mainstream American Public Etiquette." In *Meaning, Form, and Use in Context: Linguistic Applications,* edited by Deborah Schiffrin, pp. 200-209, 1984.

Kraybill, Ron. "The Mediator as Model." *Conciliation Quarterly Newsletter* 5, no. 2 (Fall 1986): 2-3.

Kupperman, Robert, and Darell Trent. *Terrorism*. Stanford, CA: Hoover Institution Press, 1979.

Laue, James H., and Gerald Cormick. "The Ethics of Intervention in Community Disputes." In *The Ethics of Social Intervention*, edited by Gordon Bermant, Herbert C. Kelman, and Donald P. Warwick, Washington, D.C.: Halsted Press, 1978, pp. 205-232.

Levdansky, Deidre. *Fundamentals of Mediating Disputes: A Manual on Mediation Training*. Pittsburgh: Pittsburgh Mediation Center, 1983.

Merry, Sally Engle, and Susan Sibley. "What Do Plaintiffs Want? Reexamining the Concept of Disputes." *The Justice Journal* 9 no. 2 (1982): 151-178.

Miller, Abraham. *Terrorism and Hostage Negotiations*. Boulder, CO: Westview Press, 1980.

Odom, Ernie. "The Mediation Hearing: A Primer." In *Mediation: Contexts and Challenges*, edited by Joseph E. Palenski and Harold M. Launer. Springfield, IL: Thomas, 1986, pp. 5-14.

Wahrhaftig, Paul. "An Overview of Community-Oriented Citizen Dispute Resolution Programs in the United States." In *The Politics of Informal Justice*, I, edited by Richard Abel. San Francisco: Academic Press, 1982.

―――. "Nonprofessional Conflict Resolution." *Villanova Law Review* 29, no. 6 (November 1984): 1463-1476.

Warren, Roland L. "Mediation of Conflicts: Some Personal Encounters." Paper given at International Society of Political Psychology, Fifth Annual Scientific Meeting, Washington, D.C., June 25, 1982.

Whitman, Joan Catherine. "Personal Value Conflict as an Ethical Dilemma in Compromise." Manuscript prepared for Philosophy Program, Northern Kentucky University, 1985.

MOVE

Adcock, Cynthia. Telephone interview with authors, Seattle, WA, April 1, 1986.

Africa, Delbert. Interview with authors, State Correctional Institute, Graterford, PA, January 12, 1987.

Africa, Jerry. Interview with authors, Philadelphia, February 22, 1986.

―――. Telephone interview, Philadelphia, May 1, 1986.

Africa, Phil. Interview with authors, State Correctional Institute, Camp Hill, PA, December 14, 1986.

Africa, Ramona. Interview with authors, State Correctional Institute, Muncy, PA, October 23, 1986.

Africa, Susan. Interview with authors, State Correctional Institute, Muncy, PA, October 23, 1986.

Albert, Sheldon. Interview with authors, Philadelphia, December 16, 1986.

Blackburne, Laura. "A Framework for Analyzing the MOVE Conflict." *Conflict Resolution Notes* 4, no. 2 (September 1986): 11-12.

Campbell, Chauncey. Interview with authors, Philadelphia, March 15, 1986.

Cox, Sharon Sims, as told to Carol Saline, 1985. "My Life in MOVE: One Woman Reveals What It Was *Really* Like." *Philadelphia Magazine.* September 1985, pp. 169-241.

Devlin, Charles. Interview with authors, Philadelphia, March 13, 1986.

Doley, Ann. Interview with authors, Philadelphia, November 20, 1985.

Farmer, Clarence. Interview with authors, Philadelphia, March 13, 1986.

Fattah, David. Interview with authors, Philadelphia, November 21, 1985.

Fattah, Sister Falaka. Interview with authors, Philadelphia, November 21, 1985.

Gaskins, Oscar. Interview with authors, Philadelphia, March 29, 1986.

Groth, Lary. Interviews with authors, Philadelphia, March 13 and 29, 1986.

Kairys, David. Interview with authors, Philadelphia, November 20, 1985.

Larsen, Robin. Telephone interview with authors, Philadelphia, April 2, 1986.

Laue, James H. "Third Party Roles in Community Conflict: The MOVE Experience." *Conflict Resolution Notes* 4, no. 2 (September 1986): 13-14.

Mitchell, Christopher. "Six Puzzles About Community Conflicts: The MOVE Situation." *Conflict Resolution Notes* 4, no. 2 (September 1986): 15-16.

Nutter, Michael A. Interview with authors, Philadelphia, March 13, 1986.

Palmer, Walter. Interviews with authors, Philadelphia, October 25, 1985, and March 25, 1986.

Philadelphia Special Investigation Commission. "The Findings, Conclusions and Recommendations of the Philadelphia Special Investigation Commission, March 6, 1986. " (Mimeographed.)

Quinn, Jim. "The Heart of Darkness." *Philadelphia Magazine* 69, no. 5 (May 1978): 128-252.

———. "They Bombed in West Philly." *Village Voice,* May 28, 1985, p. 1.

Rawls, Larry. Interview with authors, Philadelphia, September 28, 1985.
Rendell, Ed. Interview with authors, Philadelphia, February 4, 1987.
Swans, Bennie. Interview with authors, Philadelphia, October 24, 1985.
————. Telephone interview with authors, Philadelphia, April 21, 1986.
Todd, Joel. Interview with authors, Philadelphia, January 8, 1986.
————. Telephone interview with authors, Philadelphia, April 9, 1986.
Walker, Charles. Interview with authors, Concordville, PA, December 10, 1985.
Washington, Father Paul. Interview with authors, Philadelphia, March 14, 1986.

Index

adjudication, 148
Africa, Alberta Wicker, 12, 131
Africa, Birdie, 113
Africa, Chuck, 47-49, 59
Africa, Conrad, 23, 48, 56, 64, 73, 120, 127, 128, 144
Africa, Consuela, 97, 100
Africa, Davita Johnson, 97
Africa, Debbie, 12
Africa, Delbert, 11-14, 21, 47-48, 50, 51, 55, 56, 59, 64-65, 78, 80, 97, 100, 106, 108-109, 137, 138, 143, 144, 146
Africa, Ishongo, 65
Africa, Jerry, 21, 23, 26, 78, 102, 104, 105, 106, 108, 110, 120, 126, 131, 134, 135, 136, 144
Africa, John, 9, 10, 12, 14, 16, 56, 64, 136, 144, 145
Africa, Life, 23-24
Africa, Merle, 12
Africa, Patricia Brooks, 125-126
Africa, Phil, 14, 20, 23, 24, 64, 65, 74, 77, 137, 138, 144, 147
Africa, Ramona, 16, 24, 90, 104, 113, 123, 136-137

Africa, Robert, 23, 46, 48, 56, 64, 68, 73
Africa, Sandra Davis, 97, 106
Africa, Sue, 106
agreement: composting, 50, 85, 146; May 5, 1978, 37, 72, 74, 79, 81, 88, 89
Albert, Sheldon, 55, 58, 59, 67, 73, 79-80
arbitration, 148-149

Black Panther Party, 11, 19
Blackburne, Laura, 145
Blackwell, Lucien, 24
Bomb Disposal Unit, 113
Burrus, Charles, 122-123

Campbell, Chauncey, 125-126, 128, 129
Cardinal's Commission on Human Relations, 56, 63
CCCHR. *See* Citywide Community Coalition for Human Rights
Chestnut Hill, 34

About the Authors

HIZKIAS ASSEFA is associate professor of management and international affairs in the Graduate Program of La Roche College, Pittsburgh.

Dr. Assefa is the author of *Mediation of Civil Wars: Approaches and Strategies—The Sudan Conflict* (Westview Press, 1987). He has contributed many book chapters and articles in the areas of conflict resolution and crisis decision making.

Dr. Assefa holds and LL.B. from Addis Ababa University; an LL.M. from Northwestern University; and M.A. (economics), M.P.A. (public management), and Ph.D. (public and international affairs) from the University of Pittsburgh.

PAUL WAHRHAFTIG is president of the Conflict Resolution Center, Inc., in Pittsburgh and a practicing mediator.

Mr. Wahrhaftig is the editor of *Conflict Resolution Notes* and has contributed many articles to journals for the scholar and practitioner. He is one of the founders of the community conflict resolution movement in the United States.

Mr. Wahrhaftig holds a B.A. from Stanford University and a J.D. from Boalt Hall, University of California Law School.